# Did I Ever Thank You, Sister?

**A True Story**

## Sal Di Leo

Edited by Jane E. Di Leo

Sal's Book, Inc.
Minneapolis Minnesota

8/1/14
Judy:
To
wishing you
the Best

ISBN: 978-0-615-26521-6

Published by:
Sal's Book, Inc.
2611 Ulysses St. NE
Minneapolis, MN 55418
612.382.3582
www.salsbook.net

# A personal note from the author

In January of 1999, during a very cold and dark Minnesota winter, I sat down and wrote most of this story in about 6 days. It was a phone call from a newspaper reporter from Joliet, Illinois in November of 1997 that really got this whole thing started.

I wasn't intending on writing a book when I started out. I just wanted to write a story that I thought needed to be told, maybe for a little redemption or just maybe to help me reconstruct what really happened in my life so I could go on.

During the course of my journey back in time, I experienced a lot of intense emotions as the memories began to unfold in front of me. Some of them were good feelings, while others were not. I had to really take a hard look at what happened. As a result of this experience, I made some profound discoveries of events and people who have impacted my entire life, many of which I never understood until now.

I also want you to know that I do not pretend to be a writer by trade and hope you will forgive me for the mistakes you will find in this book. However, after careful consideration and feedback from some very trusted friends, I have decided not to get an official editor involved or change much of anything in this book. My daughter Jane, 17 at the time, helped do some minimal editing and we stopped there. I have been told a better writer could clean it up. But, it may lose something. Therefore, I have decided that this is my story as I have written it and will leave it that way. Since January of 1999, I have added several more chapters and again do not wish to change them. If you would please try and look beyond the errors and just read my story, I would be grateful.

Thank you.
Sal N. Di Leo

# Did I Ever Thank You, Sister?

## Dedication

To my loving wife Beth, Thank you for being my best friend forever.

To my patient children, Jane and Kate, you are the dream I have always held on to.

To my brother Mario and my sisters Maria and Kitty, I won't forget what we went through together. Your love and courage will always be appreciated forever.

To all the other wonderful people who were there for me along the way, I promise I will pass it on.

A special thanks to…

Sister Mary Paul Korman, O.S.F.
Sister Rose Spatney, O.S.F.
The Sisters Of St. Francis, Joliet, IL.
My eleven Brothers and Sisters
Rudy Raspolich Family
Dr. James P. Keenan Family
Mr. Patrick Render
Dr. Thomas G. Magruder Family
Russell and Peggy Goins
Chuck and Dorothy Weitbrecht
Mike Tvrdik
John Egan
Bud Grant, 1994 NFL Hall Of Fame
The University Of Nebraska Staff and Faculty

# Contents

# Chapter 1
## Got to go back

When we landed at Midway Airport on that cold March day back in 1998, it was about 9:30 in the morning. Mike and I had traveled from Minnesota to Chicago to attend an international corporate sponsorship convention. We were half awake.

Mike was my best friend. We had met about 10 years earlier in the antique store that my wife and I owned in an old part of Minneapolis. One day, while he was out delivering the neighborhood newspaper, for which he was also a writer and ad salesman, Mike walked into the store with his bag over his shoulder. He didn't look good and I could tell he wasn't making any money. He began by telling me his wife was in dental school, and he gave me his hardship sales pitch. During the course of our conversation, however, we discovered that we had something in common: we had both gone to school at the University of Nebraska and loved Nebraska football. He ended up selling me an ad I didn't need and couldn't afford. We became friends almost right away.

From looking at us when we got off the plane in Chicago that day, no one would have guessed we were traveling together. Even though he was more than 10 years younger than me, in his early 30s, he looked older. He was chubby, dressed like an old shoe, with half of his shirt hanging out the front of his pants and a grin on his face. I was slim, dressed in a new suit, without a hair out of place, and I had a serious look on my brow. Who would have thought he was the guest speaker at the convention and I was his guest? I looked like I should have been speaking.

"Did you rent a car?" he asked as we worked our way down toward the baggage claim. "Yep. You need a ride?" I replied. "Never thought you'd ask," he answered in his usual smart aleck way. He was always quick with a response.

"Are you going to the Welcome Banquet tonight? Good food and plenty of free drinks!" he added with a little excitement in his voice. "Maybe. If I'm back in time," I said without too much emotion. "I need to go see somebody in Joliet first," I added, while I stared ahead reading the airport signs.

"Who do you know in Joliet?" he asked. "An old nun," I said sternly. I probably wouldn't have told anyone else. But Mike was one of the few people in my life who knew my background and accepted me without question.

After I dropped off the chubby guy in front of the Hilton in downtown Chicago, I headed out. I could see him in my rear view mirror as I drove away. He was already working on the bellhop with some joke or remark. The kid was reaching for his bags, shaking his head, with a smile across his face. Mike felt it was his lot in life to make everyone laugh. He had a heart of gold to back it up, too.

Joliet was about 45 minutes south of Chicago. "Well, here goes," I thought, as I entered the on-ramp to the Interstate. "At least I have time to think a little." I was thinking about what I would find and how I would feel when I got there. A long time had passed since I left. It had been 30 years.

I could hear Simon and Garfunkel's song "The Boxer" on the radio. "Talk about timing," I said aloud as the words expressed exactly how I felt about my life: "...and he was a fighter by his trade, and he carries a reminder of every glove that kept him till cried out in his anger and his shame, I am leaving, I am leaving, but the fighter still remains...."

Finally, as I reached the edge of Joliet, I could see the old building I was looking for up on the hill. It still looked big and uninviting. I sighed deeply and turned into the long driveway.

As I worked the shiny new rental car up the winding driveway, some of the old feelings began creeping back into my mind. The large stone structure on the hill looked just as it did on the last day I was there 30 years earlier. It stood solid against the gray sky with three stories of windows looking down on the long driveway. It was as if the place had been waiting in silence over the years for me to come back and put things to rest, so it too could fade away in peace.

As I neared the uninhabited building I found myself looking up to the third-floor window where the older boys' dormitory had been, to see if maybe I was somehow still there, looking for someone to come and take me home, as I had done so many times over the six years I was there as a kid.

As the car crept up to the large stone entranceway of the orphanage, I could make out the engraved letters in the wall: "The Guardian Angel Home." My heart almost stood still as I read those words through the windshield of the rental car. I again felt the fear, pain, and shame that were associated with those words whenever anyone mentioned them when I was a kid. The gray of the day was a perfect backdrop for what I was going back to in my mind.

The old line of large cottonwood trees that lined the quarter-mile road up to the entrance hung their leafless limbs down and shook in the whipping March wind. They looked as if they had stood still in time, too, just like the building. They had always looked tired and cold in the winter, I remembered. They, too, had struggled along the way. I almost felt like they were saying, "Go away and don't ever come back. You don't need to do this."

I took a quick glance in the rear view mirror on my way out of the car to reassure myself that I was the person I was now, a well-dressed professional, just coming from a national convention at the Chicago Hilton. I needed to remind myself I had a new life now and a wonderful family, too. Somehow, however, being here made it hard to escape the thought that I might still be that orphan boy of many long and hard years past.

As I stepped out of the car and looked up at the large front entrance to the building, a cold shiver ran up my spine. I stood still, for what seemed like a year, as my mind raced with thoughts coming out of nowhere. It almost overwhelmed me. Memories of kids who were there with me—I could almost hear their voices again—and questions unanswered wanted to come together at once. It made me weak in the knees.

I somehow managed to take a deep breath and forced myself to head up the cold deserted stairs of the orphanage to the massive wooden front doors. I knew I needed to go closer and feel the building with my hands and have my body feel the steps underneath, so I could conquer this thing once and for all. I knew I needed to go back and face it. When I mounted the last of what seemed like hundreds of concrete stairs, I slowly reached for the doorbell. It rang with an echo. After several unanswered tries, I headed back to the car.

I sat for several minutes in the car and just looked up at the old building. After a while, I turned off the engine and began to remember what I had tried to push out of my mind over so many years. Old memories started unfolding in front of me like I was watching an old black-and white-movie. I didn't feel I belonged in this story.

# Chapter 2
## A long time ago

35 years earlier: 1963, Joliet, Illinois…

A dirty little boy with a shaved head of hair is staring straight up into the face an old Nun. She has her hand on his face to make sure he can't turn away while he is being scolded. While he is being scolded you can see he is uncomfortable.

"Mr. Di Leo, how many times have I got to tell you that there is no fighting in this Orphanage? There are 300 girls and boys here who have no family or place to go other than these walls and you all have to learn to live together. Like it or not. What am I going to have to do with you this time to make my point? Your sisters and brother seem to get along with everyone and are perfect role models for all of the other children," she said with a bit of anger and emotion in her voice. Then she took off on a long dissertation: "You, however, are entirely just the opposite. Just yesterday, you got thrown out of class for making smart remarks and throwing spitballs during Geography class. I think old Sister Davies is going to die one day and it will be your fault. That poor Sister should have retired years ago but she has had a place in her heart for you orphans and stayed on way past her time for a much-deserved rest. This is how your treat her. Now today, you gave Philip a black eye at lunch. What are we to do with you, Mr. Di Leo? I don't think I have ever seen a third-grade boy as bad as you in a long time. The other one ended up right here in the Joliet Penitentiary. Is that what you want?" the old nun finished.

I stood with my hands in my pockets, squirming and searching the back of my mind for any good answer I could come up with that might save me. It seemed like eternity as the larger figure of the brown-robed nun hovered over me while I searched for an answer. I knew I had used up all my good excuses and I was running out of rope. Sister Lucresia stared at me with her stern face. She barely showed any physical signs of being a human being underneath all the head gear and clothing that hid her body from the rest of the world. I was scared that this time I was

5

going to get it.

Just when it seemed inevitable that I was not going to get away with this one, Sister Nepomecine walked into the office with an important question for Sister Lucresia. It was enough to pull her away. It would buy me at least a few more moments, I thought. However, it drew her away from me until she forgot I was out there, or at least I thought she had forgotten. I was left out there until just before dinnertime. I had been there for two hours before she came back.

There was nothing I hated more than being stuck indoors after school, looking at the walls of the office with its oversized pictures of kids and angels. It was a death sentence for me. The only sounds to be heard were the ticking of the old grandfather clock and the bongs that echoed when it hit the chimes on the hour. I wanted to be outside in the apple orchard, where I could always go to hide and dream about being with my family and away from the orphanage. Even if it was March and cold, I could sit in a tree and see a long way off from the top of the hill. It was here I usually found myself wondering all over again about why my father had run off. I would relive over and over again the last time I saw him and the night he left for good, the last time we were all together as a family.

The dining hall in the orphanage was in the basement and ran across the whole length of the building on one side. A long dark corridor outside the dining hall separated the two halves of the basement. Each group of kids was escorted to their seating area with the nun who was in charge of that group of kids. The girls and boys were separated and kids were grouped according to their ages. I was in third grade and in the Little Boys group. Mario, my older brother, was in the Senior Boys group, since he was a sixth grader. My little sister Kitty, who was only 5, was in the Little Girls group, and our sister Maria was in the Junior Girls group, since she was in the fourth grade.

That night, when I entered the dining hall with the other little boys, we were the last group to be escorted in and I was at the end of the line. As we approached our tables and walked past the older boys, my brother Mario gave me a look that told me he was disappointed in me. It had gotten all over the orphanage that day that I had gotten into trouble again, and he was ashamed of me. I just stuck my head up high and walked right past his table, pretending not to care if he was mad at me.

On the other side of the dining hall we could hear the girls begin their grace before dinner. Their voices sang almost in unison, "Bless us, oh Lord, for these Thy gifts, which we are about to receive from Thy bounty, through Christ, our Lord, Amen." Their voices faded as we boys began our prayers. My troubles and needs and I were immediately lost in the number of kids in that room whose needs also must have been great and who probably also felt alone in the crowd. As I looked down toward the end of the table and saw Philip with his black eye, I felt bad for him and sorry for myself. But I was resolved to the fact that he shouldn't have called me a liar. "We really did come from a good family and our grandparents were of royal blood," I thought. My father always told us that, and I was going to defend it to the end.

That night, as I lay in the dark dormitory room with all the other little boys, lined up in our beds in rows and rows, I looked up at the ceiling late into the night. I found myself watching a soft light on the ceiling that crept in from the moon outside and was shining in our room. The winds of March whistled outside our window and sounded angry as they whipped up against the old stone structure with a vengeance.

I could hear the banging of the old radiators as the sounds came up from the bowels of the building while everyone else silently slept. I wondered if it was true when Philip had said that there were bad kids in the basement banging on the pipes to let someone know they were there and they wanted to get out. I also could not get out of my head the incident of that day and my wish that I was not there and that things could be different.

I stared for a long time into the night at the glimmering moonlight on the ceiling and I found myself making a vow I would never forget. I said, "Oh God, help me make sure that if I ever have kids someday, they never have to feel pain and be alone." The tears rushed down my face and I finally fell asleep from exhaustion.

Recess was my favorite time of the day at the orphanage. All the kids from all the groups could mix and it was almost like old times for me and my brother and sisters. Mario, Marie, Kitty and I always got together on one corner of the old blacktop in the back of the orphanage. There was an old elm tree just to the edge of the playground that we Di Leos dubbed our place, and no one else dared hang around it during recess without the risk of being thrashed by two potentially violent Sicilian boys from the poor side of town. One good look from Mario or me at a kid that just happened to pass by too close, without maybe even thinking, usually stirred their adrenaline. They sobered up quickly and picked up the pace to get the heck out of there. We seized this valuable piece of real estate by clobbering two of the biggest boys on the playground almost the first day we got there. This spot remained ours until Kitty couldn't hold on to it after I left the orphanage in 1968.

My brother and older sister were my idols and I wanted to be with them whenever I could. "You shouldn't have punched Philip in the eye," Mario said to me the next day at recess. Kitty and Marie leaned against the elm tree with their hands in their coat pockets and hummed in approval as we sat together in the back corner of the playground. "I don't care," I said. "Mom and Dad were from great families, weren't they, Mario?" I asked. "Dad always said we were from the 'House of the Lion' in Sicily. He said our name Di Leo meant 'The Lion,' didn't he Mario?" I continued to ask in desperation.

Mario and Maria were the oldest now and they understood the importance of making sure Kitty and I felt proud of our family, even if they were only in the fourth and sixth grades themselves. "Sal, Mom and Dad did come from great families," Mario said to reassure me. "Philip probably did deserve it," he added to make me feel better. But I knew even then that he didn't believe it and just wanted to make me feel okay.

"I know it's true! I am going to show everybody it's true someday," I thought with anger and desperation, even though I had doubts of my own. I understood the situation we were all in

8

on that cold March afternoon but didn't understand why. Maria, Mario, Kitty, and I hung together through those first years and tried to hold each other up the best we could. I loved them for it.

That was the way we made it through those first years. We stayed together: Mario, Maria, Kitty, and me. But, with time, things began to change in the little world we had constructed for our survival. After a year or so, our mother stopped coming to see us even once in a while on the two visiting Sundays a month the orphanage allowed. Her life seemed worse than ours. In order to go on, we began to separate our emotions from her and our father.

# Chapter 3
## Mario leaves for Boys Town

The orphanage only kept kids until they graduated from eighth grade. After that, kids were placed in foster homes, family members' homes, or institutions that took in high-school age kids. We had finally learned late in the school year that Mario was going to High School in Nebraska at a place called Boys Town. I had remembered hearing about that place somewhere before, but it seemed so far away. I don't think the four of us kids were ever really ready for that day. It came like a swift-moving summer storm in June of 1965.

"Mario, are you going to write to us from Boys Town?" I asked on that last morning we were together as we strolled across the old blacktop out behind the orphanage. It was a sunny Saturday morning in June, and Mario was about to leave in the station wagon with one of nuns to go to Chicago and fly out to Omaha, Nebraska. He was excited to be going on an airplane for the first time. I was trying to be big and brave, but I could not hold back the tears as I thought about being separated from my big brother. After all, we had been together in this situation since Dad left and I couldn't imagine being separated from him now. I didn't want to go through the pain of losing a family member again.

"Sal, it will be all right, and you have to take care of Maria and Kitty now. I'll write to you as much as I can," he said to comfort me. He was 14 and a man in life at this point, and I wanted to be big for him. As I turned my head away so he couldn't see me cry, he walked off when Sister called for him and went off to Boys Town.

That was a long day for Maria, Kitty, and me. A kid by the name of Freddy Faye, who was also in Mario's class and was going to live with an uncle in Joliet the next day, came up to me when he saw me crying off by myself. "Di Leo, don't be a big baby. Your brother wasn't a baby," he said. As he came closer to make sure I heard him, I let go one of the hardest punches I ever landed on a person's face in my life.

11

Freddy Faye had a silver-capped front tooth that was his trademark. After I hit him, I saw his lips were bleeding and he was holding his front teeth with his hand to see if I had knocked one out. He was shocked. Even though he was bigger than me and could have probably whipped me, he knew it was best to just walk away, and he did.

Later that day, the Sister who was in charge of the senior boys saw me walking around with my hands in my pockets out by the apple orchard. I was soon to be moved up to her group for the remainder of my time at the Guardian Angel Home. Sister Nepomecine, who thought a great deal of Mario, came up to me, with a rosary still in her hand. She had been out walking in the early evening after dinner and had been praying by herself when she spotted me.

Sister Nepomecine recognized I was still mourning Mario's leaving. When she got to me she said in a nice but direct voice, "Sal, almost everyone in some way is dealt a bad hand in life. The people who do the best recognize that and, with the grace of God, make the best of what they have been given. You will do well with what you have. I just know it."

That summer was hard for me without Mario around. Maria, Kitty, and I stuck together as best we could, but I found myself hanging around more with the other boys like Philip, Lyle, Ricky, and the rest of the gang. We were all moved up into the Senior Boys group and had a few more privileges.

That summer we even got a TV in our Senior Boys dormitory. That was cool, we thought, and the nuns seemed to let up on us a bit. I also started to change. Partly I was just growing older, and partly I was letting go of some of my anger at what had happened with my parents.

# Chapter 4
## School in town

The year before Mario left for Boys Town, a nun by the name of Sister Mary Paul became the new director of the Guardian Angel Home. Sister Paul was a no-nonsense kind of administrator. Immediately, she made it clear there were going to be some changes, and she made it clear that she would accept no nonsense from any of us. We were all a little scared of her at first. It wasn't long before she started to change everything and everyone knew they had better cooperate or else. I think even the other nuns who had been there for years were a bit scared of her. She was sort of a new-age nun for the orphanage at that time.

Sister Paul demanded that the only way for orphans to make it in the outside world after they left was to get them out of the orphanage for school. She also went on a fund-raising fury. She raised a great deal of money to build a new gymnasium, put together a band, and organize athletic teams to compete against other Catholic schools. She found families to take us home for the holidays so we could see what the rest of the world was like. This nun wanted us to see the world beyond the boundaries of the Guardian Angel Home. She would have made millions in this day and age in the business world. I am convinced of that to this day. But she also ruled with an iron hand and no one dared cross her.

With all the fast and furious changes brought on by Sister Paul came some problems. One of the biggest challenges she was faced with occurred when we first were sent to town to go to the other Catholic schools. The orphanage was outside the edge of town. It had a farm of its own and was surrounded by farms in those days. So Sister Paul had to go out and raise the money to buy us a bus.

It was rumored that every businessman or civic group in that community ran when they saw her coming through their front door. By the time she was finished with her fund raising, she had raised money for the new band uniforms and instruments, built the gym, gotten us the bus, purchased new school uniforms, and found tuition for 300 kids to go to the Catholic schools in town, beginning in the fall of 1965.

Since there were so many orphans that had to be placed in the Catholic schools in Joliet, it was impossible for all of us to all go to any one school. My sister Maria went to St. Pat's, and my little sister Kitty and I went to St. Raymond's. Mario had already left for Boys Town.

By the end of the summer, the anticipation of going to the schools in town had made all of us at the orphanage nervous. We didn't know what to expect. We had only gone to school with other orphans. However, one of the benefits that we were looking forward to was getting new uniforms and new shoes.

The new uniforms were the first new clothes I could remember having in my life. I was 11 years old. When a man came out from town to measure each kid that summer, it was exciting. When the big day came in September to go to school, it was unforgettable.

I remember getting out of bed extra early and feeling the excitement of putting on my new clothes. Then I went down to the dining room for breakfast with the other boys in my group. As we neared the dining room, I could hear the bustle of all of other kids who were already in there. Everyone was excited. You could feel it in the air. When we got in the door, I could see one boy in a white shirt, black pants, new shoes, and a tie. He looked great. As a matter of fact, we all looked pretty good. Even Philip, who was always a slouch, looked pretty good with his slicked-back hair and his new uniform. We all were strutting our stuff.

After breakfast, we excitedly went up to grab our stuff from our lockers and then headed out to board the new bus to ride into town. Our hearts and minds raced as we wondered about what was going to happen next. Since there was only one bus, we had to leave early and in shifts so we could all get to school on time. Maria, Kitty and I were lucky because our schools were on the same side of town and we could ride together.

During our shift, St. Pat's was the first stop. This was Maria's school. There were lots of kids outside on the playground, all in uniform, playing before the first bell rang. When Maria stepped off the bus that was clearly marked "Guardian Angel Home," many of the kids on the playground stopped playing and stared at her. I will never forget the look on Maria's face when we dropped her off. It was obvious to me and all the other kids on the bus at that instant that our short-lived excitement about our new school clothes was silly.

We knew then that getting through the first day of school in town wasn't going to be easy. Most of the kids in town had never seen an orphan, and everyone wanted to get a closer look. They crowded around Maria and the other kids from the orphanage as they got off the bus. My sister looked over her shoulder while I stared out the window at her. She was being led into St. Pat's ahead of the other kids by a nun who had been waiting just for the orphan kids. I caught the fear and the shame from Maria's look in that instant and my heart sank to bottom of my stomach.

After that first stop, you could only hear the shifting of the bus's gears as the driver pushed and pulled the large stick shift up and back. We climbed up and down hills and felt the curves as we turned corners in silence. The excitement of our new clothes wore off. We were reminded, once we left the confines of the orphanage, that we were still orphans. For the first time, I looked at the orphanage as a safe place to hide. I wanted to go back, just so I could be with kids who were in the same boat I was in.

We dropped several kids at Holy Cross and watched almost the identical situation unfold.

By the time we got to St. Raymond's, there were only four of us left on the bus—my little sister Kitty, Ricky Barker, Philip, of all people, and me—and it was quiet. It was hard to believe that I would ever take a liking to Philip, but on that day, I decided to become his friend, and if any kid in that school gave him or any of us any trouble, I would thrash that kid until he would never forget it. After all, since I had pounded Philip it was an unspoken rule at the Orphanage that I had some responsibility in looking after him. He was a fellow orphan and we had to stick together.

15

# Chapter 5
## Day one at St. Raymond's

As the bus drove up to St. Raymond's, we could immediately see a difference in this school compared with the others. The church was much bigger, the grounds were better-kept, and the school looked nicer. It was the Cathedral School for the Joliet Catholic Diocese. It was also where the rich kids in town went to school.

The warm September sun was well up now as we drove up to the school. A slight breeze was blowing through the open window next to me. I could smell breakfast being cooked in one of the beautiful houses with the elegant porches and neatly manicured yards that were next to the school. They looked happy and inviting. "I wish I lived here," I thought.

One of the benefits of being the last stop was that all the other kids had already been marched into school, since it was almost 8 a.m. School was about to start. At least we could slip in without anyone noticing, I thought. No one was on the playground waiting for us. Not even a nun could be spotted. We thought we were off the hook.

The school building was well-kept, with a Spanish-style design. Built in the 1920s, the school looked classy and clean. Inside, it was spotless with its waxed marble floors, polished brass doorknobs, and well-varnished woodwork. It smelled new as we walked down the long hallway past the classrooms.

We could hear roll call being taken by a nun at the head of each class as we passed by. Straight ahead, down the long dark hallway, a door was open. A red light above the door displayed the letters O-F-F-I-C-E. Philip, Ricky, Kitty, and I headed toward the red-lit sign. No one else could be seen in the hallway.

Just as we turned into the office, we ran right into someone who was in a hurry to get out. Philip was behind me and Ricky behind him, with Kitty bringing up the rear. In an instant I smashed right into this person and knocked her glasses off. We all piled up on top of each other like a train wreck.

Quickly realizing that I had run into a nun, I tried to apologize to her while I was reaching down to grab her glasses. I saw that they were gold wire-rimmed glasses that had very thick lenses. The Sister looked awkward and blind as she tried to pull herself back together. "Well? Who? Where in the world?" she stuttered as she tried to piece together what had just happened. "I am sorry, Sister," I said, as I handed her the glasses. "We are the kids from the "Guardian Angel Home", I added, trying to make some conversation.

"I am Sister Patrick Kelly," she said. "Your Principal," she added, with irritation in her voice. "You are late. You tell Sister Paul she will need to do a better job of getting you orphans here on time!"

"Yes, Sister," we all said together, hoping that by agreeing with her we might be able to take some of the edge off the situation.

"Well. What are your names? I need to get you to your classes," she said, without any reassurance in her voice that we were off the hook. She reached around and grabbed a clipboard and began studying it with her thick glasses.

"My name is Sal Di Leo, and this is Philip Belcher, Ricky Barker, and my little sister Kitty Di Leo," I answered, with as much confidence in my voice as I could muster.

"Let's see, you three boys are all in the sixth grade. Philip, you and Salvatore are in one sixth grade class and you, Mr. Barker, are in the other sixth grade class," she went on to say as she continued to study her list. "You, Miss Katherine, are in the third grade class of Sister Antonella. I will escort you to your classes today. Just remember them tomorrow and be on time," she finished as she began leading us down the hall.

Kitty was hanging on desperately to my hand. I could tell she was scared. "Sister," I said, "is it okay if we take Kitty to her class first?" I asked. There was no response until we were almost all the way down the hall.

"Well, Katherine, here you are," she said, as she grabbed Kitty's hand from mine and quickly led her into the already started class. "Sister Antonella," I heard her say as we listened from outside the hall, "this is the orphan girl. Her name is Katherine."

Outside in the hall, I could feel my heart race and I knew Philip and Ricky were thinking and feeling the same things I was. We just looked at the floor with our hands in our pockets. We weren't going to slip into school un-noticed as we had hoped.

When Sister Kelly came out into the hallway, not one of us said another word as we followed this old nun down the never-ending hallway. We somehow knew that each of us had to deal with this situation and face it in our own way. I could hear our footsteps on the polished marble floor echoing as we worked our way past the other classrooms with their open doors. As we got nearer to the last rooms down the hall, I felt my throat going dry, and I began breathing a little heavier. I was mad and didn't want to be on display in front of all these rich kids. I wished I could just disappear. But it was too late and there was no way that was going to happen anyway. The second-to-last door on the left was where Sister turned in, with the clipboard still in her hand.

"Salvatore and Philip, follow me," came out of her mouth and we were hustled into the room. The bright lights in the room and loud voice of Sister Robert Therese already giving instructions to the 38 other kids almost overwhelmed me.

I didn't want to look directly at anyone, but I glanced quickly out of the corner of my eye and could see the kids were bright and polished-looking in their uniforms. They sat in their desks, lined up in rows, facing forward to the front of the class where Sister Robert Therese's desk was and where we were standing at the front door of classroom.

The nun stopped giving instructions and all the noise in the room also stopped as we entered. "Sister Robert Therese, here are the orphan students, Salvatore and Philip. They were late. I instructed them to make sure they get the message back to Sister Paul at the Orphanage to be on time tomorrow."

My heart felt like it stopped at that instant and I could hardly stand there as Sister Robert Therese and all 38 kids stared at us. It seemed like forever before Sister Robert Therese acknowledged us being there and thanked Sister Rose so she could leave.

As Philip and I stood there in silence, on display in front of the class for what seemed like eternity, Sister Rose turned and abruptly headed out to take Ricky Barker to his death alone. I was sure he would run away before she could corner him, but he didn't.

"Well, who is whom?" Sister Robert Therese asked in a rather pleasant voice. Even in her nun's clothing you could see she was a much younger nun, probably in her early 30s.

I cleared my throat and answered in a broken voice, "My name is Sal and this is Philip."

"Do you go by Sal or Salvatore?" Sister Robert Therese asked kindly as she looked down at the roster in front of her on her desk.

"I don't like Salvatore and wished my parents never gave me that name," I said. At that, the other kids, who were mesmerized by the whole incident, began to laugh—I don't think out of making fun, but out of amusement. "Philip just goes by Philip," I added, feeling a little more confident.

"Well, Sal and Philip, welcome to sixth grade at St. Raymond's. You two may take a seat in the back two seats that are open."

Philip and I lumbered back to the available desks. I headed for the one by the window. I wanted to be able to look out into the morning sunshine again. I also wanted to see the beautiful houses and forget who I was for the moment.

On the way back to my desk, a pretty brown-haired girl with beautiful brown eyes caught my eye as she smiled at me. Her face seemed kind and her smile made me feel a little better right away. I would learn her name was Mary Fehrenbacker. She was to become my friend, and she was kind to me from the first day I went to St. Raymond's until I left in 1968.

Philip, meanwhile, ended up behind the biggest boy in the class and he was fine hiding there. For him, it was just what he wanted: out of sight and out of mind. We looked at each other for a moment and then tried to settle in.

# Chapter 6
## Life goes on

That first day at St. Raymond's took forever, it seemed. When the Guardian Angel Home bus finally arrived at 4 p.m. to pick up the four of us, school had been out for an hour. We were last on the route. The four of us climbed onto the bus and I sat down next to another boy who looked ahead with a blank stare on his face. Kitty found Maria and sat with her. Everyone was quiet, either looking out the window or staring off into space. I chose to look out the window.

At the dinner table that night, and until we all went to bed, there wasn't much said by anyone about that first day at school in town. We somehow knew that every one of us probably had a similar day and felt the same way. It was lonely.

That night as I lay in bed, I relived the day over and over in my head. I'm sure the other kids did, too. The bright light of the day, however, was the smile from the little brown-haired girl with the bow in her hair. The thought of her gave me something good to think about as I drifted off to sleep.

After the first week at school things got a bit easier at St. Raymond's. Some of the kids really tried to make us feel welcome, especially Mary Fehrenbacker. She introduced herself to me a few days later on the playground at recess and introduced me to some of the boys she was friends with. Philip and I even got into a basketball game out on the playground. We did all right and scored some points with the boys. We always knew, however, that we were different, especially when they picked teams. It wasn't until the third or fourth game that someone would finally pick us, out of kindness or maybe sympathy. But we were pretty good players, too, and as time went along that out-pulled our being different. After all, winning was winning to the boys in the sixth grade at St. Raymond's in 1966.

My friendships at St. Raymond's grew, and I began to understand how the kids from good families thought. Eventually, most of the kids at St. Ray's were accepting of the kids from the orphanage. The kids at St. Ray's were pretty decent kids for the most part. I learned a lot from them about what it means to have goals and to be secure (even though I was not).

At the orphanage, I found myself less likely to get into fights, and I started thinking more about just getting on with my life. One good thing that happened was that Kitty and I were taken home for the holidays by a wonderful family by the name of Raspolich.

The Raspoliches were a big Catholic family that had a bunch of kids and lived out in the country. They had horses, too. We spent many holidays thereafter with them. Kitty and I got to see how a real family functioned.

The two oldest boys, Rudy Junior and Rodney, became like brothers to me. We did a lot of riding, shooting BB guns, swimming in the creek, and building forts. I am indebted to Rudy Senior and Beverly Raspolich for sharing their family with Kitty and me. They made my last years at the Guardian Angel Home so much better.

# Chapter 7
## Philip's secret

Not long after school started in the fall of 1965, the rest of the world found out that Philip had a secret. The kids and teachers at St. Raymond's found out by surprise one day. All of us at the orphanage already knew about it, but we never thought much about it. The nuns had discovered it in the fourth grade at our school at the orphanage.

Philip had been in the orphanage from the time he was 6 years old. (I arrived about the time we were both in third grade.) His mother and his little sister always came to visit him on visiting Sunday.

I remember seeing the three of them together on one of my first visiting Sundays at the orphanage and thinking how strange they appeared. No one from my family came, so I was curious to see what the other kids' families looked like.

I learned that Philip's mother and sister rode the Greyhound bus down from Chicago, which was about 40 miles away, to visit him. What really struck me as peculiar, though, was that they never left the grounds like all the other kids and their families. Instead, his mother always had a lunch packed and the three of them would wander off into the apple orchard or find some other place to sit.

Once they found a place to be alone, they would read books together all day long until it was time for Philip's mom and sister to go. I don't think I ever saw them say one word the whole time I watched them. I thought it was strange to sit and read and not talk to each other.

In the third grade, in the school at the orphanage, Philip would always sit in the back of the room with a book in his lap, reading while a nun was teaching. He was constantly caught, reprimanded, and had extra work thrown at him. Somehow, however, he always managed to know the answers to the difficult geography or math questions when he was put on the spot by a teacher who caught him reading instead of paying attention to her in class. It was then that I began to realize that he was different.

One day in November of the fourth grade at the orphanage, while we were in afternoon math class, I found out that Philip was more different than I thought. I remember hearing a knock at the door during that same class. I can't remember the name of the nun who was teaching math, but she had just had a tussle with Philip.

While she was trying to show us how to solve a difficult problem on the blackboard, she spotted Philip with a book under the desk in his lap. I remember that nun almost losing it and storming toward Philip's desk with the pointer in her hand. "Philip is going to get killed," I thought.

When Sister arrived at his desk she said, "All right, Mr. Belcher, give me the book." Philip reluctantly handed over to her the largest hardcover book I had ever seen in my life. My eyes could hardly believe how thick it was. The nun could barely grab the book with one hand because it was so thick and heavy.

When she finally got hold of it and studied the title on the cover, I remember seeing her face turning even redder. "'War and Peace'? Where did you get this book?" she asked, in almost a shocked way. I had no idea what that book was about. My only thought was that maybe it was a bad book and Philip was really going to die.

She threw the book down on her desk in disbelief with a loud thump. She then said, "Mr. Belcher, since you have not been paying attention in my class, I do not believe you understand the lesson I have been teaching." She was pointing to a rather complicated long division problem that she had written on the blackboard.

Before she could continue to work on Philip, he walked up to the blackboard with his lumbering shuffle, picked up the chalk, and filled in the answer. The disbelief on that nun's face and on the faces of the other students still sticks in my mind. It was just then that the knock at the door came.

It was Sister Lucresia, who was still the Head Nun at the time. President John F. Kennedy had just been shot, and we were going to the chapel upstairs to pray for him. Philip was saved for the moment. However, I remember it as a sad day for us at the orphanage and for America. We all cried over the death of our President, who was so young and handsome.

Soon after, the nuns realized that Philip might have a gift, and they began taking him outside the orphanage to get tested. On one occasion, I remember looking out the window and watching him get into a long black car and riding off. The nuns told us he was going to Chicago to get tested. None of us ever truly heard the results of his test, but we knew he was exceptional, even if we thought he was weird sometimes.

Two years later, the kids and teachers in the sixth grade at St. Raymond's found out about Philip's secret in almost the same manner. It happened about the middle of the second week of school, again during math class. The incident was almost identical to what happened at the orphanage: Philip was caught reading a book under his desk during the "New Math" (as they called it then) class and went up to the front of the room and whizzed through the problem on the blackboard. The kids and the nun were as mesmerized as I had been back at the orphanage in fourth grade.

It never made sense to me that the nuns at St. Raymond's didn't know about his gift until that incident. However, after that, Philip went for special math classes at the College of St. Francis, a few blocks away. His math scores were the highest in the state of Illinois until we graduated from eighth grade in 1968. Philip had earned some respect for us orphans with that, too, and I liked him for it.

For me, school went pretty well. I made a couple of pretty good friends, and I managed to make it through without getting thrown out for fighting or something. However, as the spring of 1966 came, I began to worry about what was going to happen that summer at the orphanage. It was the worst thing I could possibly imagine, and it was going to happen again. I found myself waking up many mornings with a terrible feeling in my stomach. It was hard to get going many times that spring from the worry I kept inside me.

# Chapter 8
## Maria leaves

In the summer of 1966, my sister Maria graduated from eighth grade. It was just Kitty and me then. As worried as I had been, I found that I wasn't as traumatized at the loss of Maria as I was with the loss of Mario.

It was easier for me to let go of Maria because she was adopted by a wealthy family right there in Joliet for her high school years, and I knew we would see her. Also, since she was a girl, I hadn't spent as much time with her. My little sister Kitty took it very hard, though. After Maria left, Kitty always seemed scared and a bit withdrawn.

I don't think I was much help for Kitty with her little-girl needs, and I regret not being there for her as much as I could. I tried, but I just didn't give as much as I should have to her.

One day, after Maria had left, I found Kitty out by the old elm tree, crying. She was still a little girl, only 9 years old, and I was moved by her crying. "Kitty, what's wrong?" I asked as I held her. "I miss Mario and Maria," she said. "Then, you will be leaving me, too," she added.

"Don't worry about that. Maria is right here in town and I am not leaving for two years," I told Kitty reassuringly. But I didn't make any effort to spend a whole lot of time with her. Thank goodness for the Raspolich family. We were able to have great times together during the holidays, at least.

No one dared mess with Kitty though, because they knew they would cross me. That was a given, and unfortunately for one kid whose name I cannot remember, my point was displaced on his forehead during the summer Maria left.

During that summer of 1966 a good thing happened, too. Mario came back to Illinois from Boys Town for a week and stayed at our older sister Angie's place just outside Chicago in Waukegan, Illinois. It was a great week.

Kitty and I went up to Angie's to stay with him. Angie was much older than those of us who went into the orphanage. She was about 20 years older than Kitty. The second oldest of the 12 children in our family, Angie had long been on her own when our father ran off. When mom stopped coming to see us at the orphanage, Angie took up the role of trying to be a mother to us, in addition to taking care of her own family. She would come and get us for the holidays once in a while, or for a week in the summer. She worked hard at trying to make us not feel alone.

That summer when Mario came back from Boys Town, I couldn't believe how much he had changed over his freshman year in high school. He was bigger, stronger-looking, and had grown up a lot. I noticed right away that he kept more inside of himself and seemed more thoughtful. I asked him a lot of questions. He didn't say much about Boys Town except that it was tougher than the orphanage.

The first night he was home, we all bombarded him with a million questions. He finally went to bed about 9:30 p.m., exhausted from his trip and from all of us pulling on him. I was so glad to see him.

The next day, I was sitting outside in Angie's back yard, and Mario had just finished mowing Angie's lawn. He came over to sit by me. Kitty was still in bed and I was glad to be with him alone. The morning sun sent the shadows of the small trees in the back yard away from us as it rose over the front of the house. The smell of fresh-cut grass was everywhere. I loved that smell. It was a peaceful summer morning, and summer always made me happy.

"Mario, what's Boys Town like?" I asked after we sat there for a while. "Well, Sal, it's harder there than where you are now. There are some really tough kids in Boys Town from all over, especially some of the kids from Kansas City or California. You have to be a good fighter to make it and learn to keep your mouth shut. But I have some good friends and we stick together," he said.

I didn't like what I heard, but I knew I was still two years away from the possibility of going there anyway. That was all Mario ever said about Boys Town, and he let me know he didn't want to talk any more about it during his vacation.

28

Anyway, it was a great week with Mario, and then he went back to Boys Town. I didn't cry this time as much as I had when he left the first time. I guess I was getting used to the separation. Kitty cried a lot. She was very sensitive that summer after Maria left the orphanage.

# Chapter 9
## My final stretch at the orphanage

My seventh- and eighth-grade years seemed to blur together. Nothing really sticks out as too bad or exceptionally good.

As adolescence set in, the boys noticed the girls a little more and the girls noticed the boys more. Some of the kids began to try the boyfriend and girlfriend stuff. That was uncomfortable for me. Even if I did like a girl at St. Ray's, there was no way I could see her after school or go to any functions with her because I had to go back to the Guardian Angel Home every night and weekend. Even though I secretly thought a great deal of Mary Fehrenbacker, I knew better than to let her know that. She was always so kind to me, and I figured I wasn't good enough for her anyway. I didn't want to ruin a good friendship. It was better that way. I'm not sure she ever knew my feelings for her. I probably would have scared her to death.

Philip Belcher, as expected, tested out as the smartest kid in the state of Illinois in eighth grade. I continued to become less dependent on my family's memories and more focused on just getting through the best I could at the orphanage and at St. Raymond's.

One of the most significant things that happened to me probably went unnoticed by everyone else at St. Raymond's and the orphanage. But it had an impact on me.

I was asked by Sister Robert Therese to be one of the speakers for our eighth-grade gathering on the last day of school. I was surprised and extremely happy about the opportunity. "Sister," I said when she offered it to me, "there are a lot of other kids in our class who are smarter and who could speak better than I can."

"Maybe. But you are going to do something great someday and I am proud of the way you finished up here," she said.

Sister Robert Therese was our teacher from fifth through eighth grade. She had followed us all the way through. She was also very tolerant of me. I don't know why. But in this particular instance, she must have wanted to give me something special to go out with. It touched me a great deal to be able to participate on that level.

So that's how I got to speak at the ceremony a few weeks prior to our actual graduation night activities. One of the Illinois state senators came to this event. My little speech was titled, "Do you know where we are going to be in the year 2000?" It must have been okay, because no eggs or tomatoes landed on my head. But, most importantly, I felt special. It took my confidence level to a new height.

On the night of our actual eighth-grade graduation in June 1968, the kids all looked so happy, and they were wonderfully dressed. Mary Fehrenbacker, Maureen Kremeens, Sue Robinson and all the other girls looked beautiful in their lovely dresses. Bruce Sickta, Bill Whitley, Gary Cheek, Mike Tracy, Teddy Codo, and the other guys were all dressed in their suits and they looked pretty cool.

Even those of us from the orphanage looked great that night, I thought. Philip, Ricky, and I had our suits, too. Even if they weren't new, we thought we looked pretty cool. Sister Paul bought us each a corsage to wear on our suits. It was the first time I had ever seen a corsage, and it was neat to have it on when we arrived at the church like everyone else did.

Philip's mother and his little sister rode the Greyhound bus in from Chicago so they could be there on his graduation night. Ricky Barker's family came and they looked great, too. I wrote to my mother to see if she could make it, but she never showed up. However, Sister Paul came to be there for me.

It was a great night whether I was alone or not. I knew I was with a great bunch of kids, and somehow I felt I was almost as good as they were that night. I also knew I would probably never see any of them again. They were all going on to Joliet Catholic High School (the boys) or Joliet Catholic Academy (the girls). I would be leaving for Boys Town in two days.

I took a good look around me that night and felt grateful that it had all worked out at St. Raymond's. I was very appreciative that I had gone to school there after all. It was a night to remember.

The next morning, while I was listening to my 6-transistor radio out back on the old blacktop behind the orphanage, I heard a terrible piece of news on the radio. The night before, on our graduation night, Senator Robert Kennedy had been shot and killed in California during his presidential campaign. I felt sick to my stomach and couldn't understand why. I couldn't believe another Kennedy had been killed.

Sister Robert Therese was an Irish Catholic nun who loved the Kennedys. She was a very politically aware nun and she made it a point to make us all very politically aware. Vietnam was in full swing in 1968, and the United States was almost at civil war. We learned a great deal about politics from her.

On that particular morning I was to ride with one of the other nuns over to St. Raymond's to pick up my stuff from my locker at school. When we got to St. Ray's, I went over to the Sisters' Convent House on the grounds there, and knocked on the door.

Another nun came to door. "Sister, is Sister Robert Therese here?" I asked. The nun recognized me from school and said, "She's just finishing her breakfast. Who are you?"

"My name is Sal Di Leo and I am one of the kids from her class from the Guardian Angel Home," I answered. "Just a minute," she said, and she went back inside.

As I stood out by the back door of the convent, I looked around again at the pretty homes of the neighborhood by St. Raymond's. I had the transistor radio to my ear and I was still listening to the news to get updates on the Kennedy assassination. The birds were chirping, the sun was shining. It seemed such a peaceful day for such bad news.

When Sister Robert Therese came to the door, I could see she still had a napkin tucked under her belt, and she looked confused to see me there. "Sal, what can I do for you?" she asked.

"Sister, I know how much you like the Kennedys," I said slowly, "but I didn't know if you knew that Bobby Kennedy was shot and killed last night out in California."

A shocked look came over her face and finally she said, "Oh my God! Not Bobby!" I could see she was beginning to cry and she excused herself. I always felt bad about being the one to tell her, and I wished I never had. I'm not sure why I told her in the first place. Maybe I just wanted to feel important and be the one with the big scoop. It backfired.

The next day I woke early at the orphanage and went to early Mass. I sat with Kitty and for the first time I was really worried about her. I also began to regret not being able to be with her anymore and wished in my mind that I had spent more time with her. She had her curly black hair in a bow and just sat as close to me as possible. She was going into the fifth grade and seemed so little to me still. I prayed for her and hoped she could make it alone. I tried to reason with myself and reminded myself that Maria was close. But I wasn't convinced.

After Mass, Kitty and I ate breakfast together and then it was time for me to go. Ricky Barker, Philip Belcher, and I were leaving for Boys Town. Inside I was excited about being able to be with Mario again. I was also sad to leave Kitty behind.

As we walked out to the car together, Kitty was crying the biggest tears I had ever seen. I couldn't look at her very well. I just told her I loved her and that she would be all right. As the car pulled away from the old blacktop with Sister Nepomecine at the wheel, I waved to Kitty and saw an old Sister standing with her. I didn't feel the way I thought I would feel when the day finally came to leave the Guardian Angel Home. I thought about the night that my dad left and the day we went to the orphanage. It all seemed a blur, and I wasn't sure how I felt.

When we finally got to O'Hare Airport in Chicago, I got excited again. Philip, Ricky, and I were going to fly to Omaha. I had never been on an airplane before. As we boarded the plane, I turned around to look at Sister Nepomecine and said, "Thank you, Sister." She said, "Take care of yourself and Mario."

# Chapter 10
## On my way to Boys Town

As we took off from O'Hare Airport on our way to Omaha and Boys Town, I was glad Philip and Ricky were with me. We had been foxhole buddies, so to speak, for a long time, and I was kind of attached to them by now. I felt we could do well at Boys Town if we stuck together. I remembered what Mario had said about Boys Town being so rough and how important it was to have good buddies.

I looked out the window almost the whole trip while Philip read a novel and Ricky slept. On the trip I relived a lot of things in my mind about the past years at the orphanage, and I kept thinking about Kitty.

When we finally got above the clouds it was an unbelievable experience for me. When I used to look up into the sky from the top of an apple tree in the orchard at the orphanage, I wanted to be in the clouds. I felt that was what heaven would be like. Now I was looking down on them. They seemed different. "Maybe I'm different now," I thought as we traveled on.

"Hey, Philip, you think you and I will be bunk mates here?" I asked as we landed in Omaha. "Mario says everybody sleeps on bunk beds at Boys Town," I added. I was trying to act like I was an expert on Boys Town to impress him and Ricky.

"Maybe," he said with a little excitement in his voice, too. He was trying to show he appreciated me thinking we were going to be buddies at Boys Town.

Ricky kept to himself. He was sad because he left behind two sisters and he was very close to them. His older brother Bill was in Mario's class at the orphanage, and Bill went to Boys Town with Mario. "Hey, Ricky. I'll bet you'll be glad to see Bill again," I added, to get him into the conversation. Then I saw he had puffy eyes and had been crying. "That's why his head was turned away from us most of the trip out here," I thought.

"Sure," he said. I didn't say much more to him after that until we got to Boys Town.

When we got off the plane, a guy in his late 20s wearing

a Boys Town sweatshirt was waiting for us. His name was Mr. Barberschmidt. He seemed nice and got us to the van outside with our luggage. We each had a footlocker trunk with our stuff in it. We loaded up and headed out to Boys Town. Like the orphanage, Boys Town was located several miles outside of town.

Mr. Barberschmidt turned out to be the head counselor of the Orientation Center at Boys Town. This was a temporary housing area on the grade school side of Boys Town. (The grade school side was also the original site of Boys Town.) The Orientation Center was where they put the new kids until they figured out where they were going to be placed permanently.

Boys Town in 1968 was divided up into two major groups of kids. They separated us according to grade school kids and high school kids living in separate sections. The grade school kids lived in the dormitories, and the high school kids lived in the cottages. The buildings on the grade school side were built back in the late 1930s and early 1940s, while the cottages, which looked like pleasant little homes, were built in the early 1960s.

When we finally drove up to Boys Town, I couldn't believe how big it was as we worked our way through the grounds. We passed the famous statue of the kid with his little brother on his shoulders, on through until we reached the Orientation Center.

When we got there, it was about noon and the kids on the grade school side were lining up to go in for lunch as we passed by the grade school dining hall. I could immediately see a difference in the kids here. They looked big, mean, and tough. There were no girls, and I saw a lot of black kids. There had never been black kids at the orphanage.

I began to realize I had softened over the years at the orphanage, and I was scared. I again remembered what Mario had said about the differences between Boys Town and the orphanage.

Mr. Barberschmidt quickly parked the van and told us to leave our gear in the van until after lunch. "We're going to catch lunch just in time," he said. Philip, Ricky, and I followed him through the front door. When we got inside I really noticed a difference between Boys Town and the orphanage. There were at least 300 boys, at rows and rows of tables, all talking at once.

The place looked rather dirty and dingy. As we were escorted to the front to the orientation table, we passed by table after table of mean-looking boys. "Hey, look, new sissies," some kid said as we worked our way to the front. Each table had a male counselor at one end and about 30 kids sitting with him. I was surprised when we didn't say grace.

About eight kids were already at the orientation table with a young man about 17 years old at the table with them. The young man at the end of the table was cleanly dressed, with his blond hair slicked back. It turned out he was a senior in high school, and he was our "commissioner," as they called them at Boys Town. On the high school side, each cottage had a junior or senior boy who was the commissioner. He was in charge of the house, along with the adult counselor. The commissioners were elected by the other kids and appointed by the counselors.

Ken Shorter was this fellow's name, and he had a special appointment to be the Orientation Center's commissioner. One of the privileges of this position was that he was allowed more time to go to town and get off the grounds. He had to have a special disposition to deal with new kids of all ages at the Orientation Center, especially since kids were so homesick for the two weeks they were there.

The Orientation Center was actually quite new and nice. It was set up to handle about 50 kids at a time, but while we were there, there were never more than about 14 kids. This made it more relaxing for the counselors, and they were able to give each of us more time. Orientation was not a bad stint, but I knew we had to get out and live with those other boys soon. That thought bothered me, but I knew I had to deal with it.

Two days passed before I got to see Mario. I told him I didn't know where they were going to place me, but I wanted to be in the Choir Section because I heard they went on tours and got out of Boys Town for an 8-week tour of the country every year. As a matter of fact, the world-famous Boys Town Choir was in Japan right then.

"Sal," Mario said, "don't ask for the choir. There are some strange kids over there and most of the rest of Boys Town doesn't like them."

It was too late. "The paper work has already started," a counselor told me when I asked for a change about a week later. I should have asked sooner, but I couldn't get the idea of taking long trips out of my mind. I should have listened to Mario.

Mr. Barberschmidt and Ken proved to be kind and sensitive. Ken was an unusual young man, but I liked him. At night he would play Beethoven, Bach, and other classical music on the record player for us. He really loved it. We would also see him reading all the time. It wasn't long before he and Philip were sitting around listening to classical music in the rec room and reading. Ken didn't seem like he fit into Boys Town. I think that was why he probably really chose to be a commissioner of the Orientation Center.

Ricky Barker and I spent a great deal of time fighting Ken and Philip for different music on the record player, and the two of us played a lot of ping-pong while the two nerds read. All in all, it was a pretty good stay in the Orientation Center for those two weeks. Philip and I were bunkmates after all. He got the top bunk. I let him.

Ken mentioned one day that he came from Ohio as a junior and had only been at Boys Town about a year. He said he really missed Ohio. About three months later, in September, I learned that Ken had run away from Boys Town, and I never heard from him again.

# Chapter 11
## Hell in the Choir Section

Philip and Ricky were placed together and I was going to be alone in the Choir Section. I was being sent to Building No. 3 on the grade school side and they were going to Building No. 2. We thought we would go to the high school side right after orientation. We didn't know we were going to have to stay on the grade school side until there were openings in the cottages on the high school side, due to the overflow of kids. That bothered us a lot, but we had no choice.

I think we were all nervous on that last day of orientation as we packed our trunks again. "Hey, Philip, I'll be right next door to you guys," I said, to reassure him as well as myself. He didn't reply, but kept on packing.

The most noticeable difference between Boys Town and the Guardian Angel Home was the uneducated male counselors. Somehow, I missed the affection the nuns gave us right away, and I wished the place was cleaner. I didn't really think the nuns were very affectionate when I was at the orphanage. But I soon noticed the men counselors didn't pay attention to our emotional needs as much and didn't really give a damn anyway.

The "you've got to be tough to make it here, boy" attitude was encouraged by the counselors, and the kids carried the torch. It was obvious to me, also, that the education of the counselors was lacking compared to the nuns, who had at least college degrees and in many cases master's degrees. The nuns encouraged education and the Boys Town counselors encouraged sports. I didn't like the difference.

On the grade school side of Boys Town, where Philip, Ricky, and I found ourselves, there were four buildings where most of the kids were housed. I was in the choir building, and Philip and Ricky were right next door to us. I rarely saw them after the first day we were separated, except for a second in the dining hall and in class during summer school, which everyone had to attend and which started later that month.

It was obvious from the beginning that Mario was right

about the Choir Section. Building No.

3 had its own eating section in the dining hall and its own class schedule during summer school. We spent a great deal of time in the music hall or chapel working on singing. The other significant difference was that the choir was almost a clique with its own pecking order from the little kids on up to the big kids. The choir counselors and Father Schmidt, the priest who had made the choir famous over the 20 years it had been in existence, treated the kids according to their loyalty to the choir and their ability to sing. Father Schmidt and the counselors turned their backs on a lot of inappropriate behavior if you were good in the choir. The first night I was in Building No. 3, I found out how the system worked.

When I moved into Building No. 3 that first day, a kid by the name of Bill Bagley, who had been in Boys Town for at least eight years already (he was my age), met me at the door. Bill was a big, nice kid who for some reason took a liking to me. Maybe because when I found out his name was Bagley, I called him "Bacho Galupo," which in Italian means "Bagley," I told him. I'm not sure where I came up with that, but it worked.

Bags (as we called him) took me over to my bunk in a rather unkempt dormitory, compared to the one at the orphanage, and he found a bed for me over by the door, not far from him. He told me to hide any valuables I had or give them to the counselors. Finally he warned me to be careful at night. I didn't understand what he meant by "careful at night" except I thought it meant to watch out for thieves.

At the orphanage we didn't have much trouble with thievery. If a kid did take something, he usually got caught and got in enough trouble that the problem usually stopped right away.

Anyway, Bags and I talked a lot that day and got to know each other. He introduced me to his little brother Charlie, who looked like a modern-day Huck Finn and who had been in Boys Town almost since birth. Both Bagley kids were good-hearted, and you couldn't help but like them, even if they did appear at times to be a bit rough on the edges. I guess I had gotten used to the more refined kids at St. Raymond's and knew the difference.

However, I saw the sincerity in Bags. It was also good to have a friend like him. He was the biggest kid in the place.

After dinner and our evening of watching television that first night, it was time for lights out. Unlike the warm Orientation Center feeling or even the dorm at the orphanage, our Building No. 3 dorm room seemed lonely and cold. I remember lying down and the counselor coming in to do head count to see if everyone was in bed. There were no prayers like we said at the orphanage. We just went to bed.

When the lights finally went out, I really began to feel alone again, like I did those first nights at the orphanage. I remember looking at the ceiling until late into the night.

It must have been about 2:00 in the morning or so, when I was almost asleep, that I got the shock of my life. I felt someone trying to get into my bed from behind me. At first I didn't realize what was going on. Then I felt the breath of the person on the back of my neck and someone's hand on my back.

In shock, I wheeled around and saw a large ugly face right next to mine. I let go a yell and then pushed this person off the bed. When he tried to get back into the bed with me by force, he found out quickly that I knew how to fight and it wasn't going to be easy for him. I let go a flurry of punches on his face and kicked him in the stomach. I heard him hit the floor, cursing and telling me I was a bitch and he was going to kill me. When he came back at me again I was up on the bed and I hit him with an elbow in the mouth that sent him wheeling to the floor with a yelp.

By this time Bags was up with the lights on. He grabbed the kid by the throat and told him he would kill him if he didn't get back into his own bed. I was so shocked and upset, I didn't have time to cry. I was grateful for Bags and I was horrified by what had just happened. I never knew before then that things like this could happen. I wanted out of Boys Town.

The counselor on duty that night heard the commotion and came down to see what had happened. I was taken back by his nonchalant attitude about the incident. He just told us to get back in bed. Then in a rather light voice he told the kid to stay away

41

from me.

I did not sleep the rest of the night except for a few minutes here and there. A younger boy who was a few beds down from me was the kid's next victim about an hour later. The other boy didn't fight though and I listened with disgust as the kid took advantage of the boy. I was sick to my stomach. I couldn't cry, though. "I'm going to run away as soon as I can. I'll get back to Illinois and go to Angie's place," I thought.

The next morning, when we got up to get ready for breakfast, Bags was up first. He told me to follow him into the bathroom. He asked me if I was all right. I didn't have much to say except I thanked him for helping me. When we came out to make our beds, Bags told the kid next to him to move over to my bunk and exchange with me. The other kid I remember hesitated just long enough to see Bags look like he was going to get mad. I got my stuff as soon as I could and moved over next to Bags.

I made it clear to the kid from the night before when I walked by him that I didn't need Bags to protect me from him, and if I ever saw him near me, I would take his face off. Even though he was a big, strong kid, he knew I meant business and he didn't attempt to bother me sexually again. The word got around that even though I was small, I was tough and not a fag.

When I had a chance to confront the head counselor of Building No. 3 about the incident, he didn't do a thing. The kid was a good choirboy. I did not like the way they gave unusual treatment to the Concert Choir kids. I lost all respect for that staff, and I never got along from the beginning as a result. On many occasions I felt I was a marked man by the head counselor from then on. I was a "snitch."

# Chapter 12
## Getting by at Boys Town

On occasion, I would see Mario and some of his buddies at school and that always made me feel better. Mario had a great bunch of friends who were nice kids, and they gave me hope. Mario also reminded me that when I got down to the high school side it would get better. I never told him about that incident that first night in Building No. 3. I always felt ashamed and felt I should have listened to him.

I would see Philip and Ricky outside on occasion. One day, I went over to Philip's building to see if I could visit with him. When a kid came to the door to answer, he recognized me from the choir and told me to go away. I told him I wanted to talk to Philip Belcher. I noticed that their building looked cleaner inside and better decorated than Building No. 3. Most of the kids in their building looked a little better groomed too.

"Belcher got in trouble and is pushing a shiner right now," the kid told me. A shiner looked liked a mop with a 20-pound weight on the head. It was used to polish floors after they were waxed. They felt very heavy when you pushed one for an hour or so. That was a standard Boys Town punishment.

"Well, when can I see him?" I asked. "Never," the kid replied.

That night at dinner though, I volunteered to be a waiter. Waiters went up to get the trays of food for the tables. It was great at times when you wanted to get over and see someone at another table. As I passed closer to Philip's table I could see he had a black eye and looked rather distraught. I felt sad and mad. "I hate this place," I thought.

"Philip. What happened?" I asked as I passed by. "Nothing," he replied and just looked down. The other boys at the table heard me ask him. One boy told me, "Get your choir ass out of here."

The rest of that summer was tough. Somehow I got through it. Maybe thanks in part to Bags or maybe just because I learned to toughen up and make it through. I felt a change coming over

43

me, however. I remember seeing Mr. Barberschmidt one day bringing some new boys into the Orientation Center, and I remember thinking how much of a sissy he looked like in comparison to the counselors I had. I also remember smarting off to him one day in front of a group of new kids who were with him. He acted a bit hurt. I don't know why I did it.

One day, toward the end of the summer, I discovered that I was angry again, just like I was when I first went to the orphanage. I found out from Ken Shorter in a roundabout way, before he ran away that September.

I was passing by Ken with a group of new kids out by one of the ball fields one day. I made a remark of some kind to one of the kids Ken was with. I can't remember what it was I said, but I do remember Ken's response when he heard me.

Ken excused himself from the other kids, came up to me and looked real hard directly in my face for a few seconds, and finally said, "You don't need to become just like the rest of the bad kids here to survive. You can be the kid who came here a good kid. You've changed, Sal."

Ken's statement really hit home inside because I knew he was right. I said something in defense of my behavior in front of the other kids I was playing with to kind of cover up. But, inside, I was ashamed of myself.

Later on, when I was by myself, I thought long and hard about what I had done and what Ken had said. I found myself reflecting back to what Sister Nepomecine had said to me years earlier when Mario left the Orphanage: "Everybody is dealt a bad hand in life. But the people who do the best recognize that and do the best with what they have been given." After that incident, I decided I needed to try and grow up some more, without the anger.

That September brought great news for me, Bags, and several other freshmen who were still on the grade school side. We were being moved to the Choir Section of the cottages. "Hallelujah," I said as loud as I could when we got the news. When I saw Philip and Ricky outside, I told them I was being moved. They looked happy for me, but it would probably be next summer before they were moved. I was sad for them, but I was glad I could be closer to Mario.

Being on the high school side was a much better experience. I got to see Mario in the dining hall and go over to his cottage in Section One a lot. I also got to know his buddies. Some of his friends were the best kids I have ever met. They were not only good athletes, but good students. They were an unusual group of kids in that class of 1969 at Boys Town. Vietnam was full-blown then, and I think these kids knew in the backs of their minds that their time was running out. I also think that they were also just good kids, sort of the last of the old Boys Town kids from days past, who I heard were pretty decent people. I didn't see much of that in my class on down, however. I'm not sure why.

Several of Mario's friends had younger brothers the same age as I was and the older brothers matched us up. For the first time, I began to make friends outside the choir group, and I liked most of these kids better. We hung together in school and for the most part we were in all the top classes. There were about 10 of us that hung together, and when Philip moved down to the high school side, he was in right away. After all, Boys Town found out how smart he was, too. Philip got respect for his intelligence from the teachers, the educated counselors, and the smarter kids.

On the first day I moved down, Mario gave me some good advice. "Sal," he said, "go out for every sport you can and join every club in school. You can get out of here more often if you do. Chances are you can meet some nice girls, too."

I took Mario's advice to heart since I would not make the Concert Choir (traveling choir) my first year. As a matter of fact, as a freshman, we were only allowed to get one pass a month to get out of Boys Town. It was terrible on an adolescent boy. So I joined everything in sight. I was determined to see the outside world where I thought I belonged. I wanted to be with other kids in other high schools like the good kids I had left behind at St. Raymond's in Joliet. I didn't want to be left behind in the confines of Boys Town and it's self-made society where toughness and ignorance were the norm.

45

# Chapter 13
## I wish I had a girlfriend

On the one Saturday a month freshmen got a pass, we were given $4 and dropped off by our blue Boys Town buses in downtown Omaha from 10 a.m. until 6 p.m. You can imagine how the people in downtown Omaha felt when they saw a large number of Boys Town boys arrive on Saturdays. You can also imagine the hormones that were flying on that bus from the boys who hadn't seen a girl for a month.

My first pass was in September. We rode the bus in and it took about a half an hour. When Bags and I got closer to downtown, we decided we were going to hang together. As we got down town, I saw all the people out in the streets staring at our bus. It reminded me of my first day back at the "Guardian Angel Home" when we first went to the Catholic schools in town. We were marked and I didn't like it.

As we got off, the boys just hustled in every direction at almost a running pace. "Be back here by 6 p.m. sharp or you'll be counted AWOL!" the counselor on the bus yelled as the bus drove off.

The freedom of being on our own that first pass was almost overwhelming. I looked at the girls walking by and hoped I could meet one. Some of the older boys actually had girls meeting them there. But when I took a good look at the girls who were waiting for them, I noticed right away that they looked pretty loose. Most of them were dressed in sleazy outfits, with too much makeup on, and most were overweight.

"We've got to hustle our asses off to find some pussy," Bags informed me as we stepped off the bus. "Well, you go ahead, Bags," I said. "I'll probably see you around."

I couldn't help but feel lousy when he said that. The thought of one of those girls on the corner being my girl bothered me. My idea of a girl went back to Joliet. I was thinking of the one with the long brown hair, who looked clean and pretty, and who was kind and intelligent.

I had $4 in my pocket and some change. So I headed up the

street and just walked for hours.

Even though I was hungry by about noon, I kept thinking of Mary Fehrenbacker and the kids back at St. Raymond's in Joliet. It seemed like years since I had seen them. For the first time, I was really thinking about them. I began to get homesick for the orphanage and wished I was back in Joliet.

As I wandered along the streets of downtown Omaha, I wrestled with the thought of maybe calling Mary, but I thought she would think I was strange to do so. After all, she wasn't my girlfriend, just a kind friend.

Before leaving Boys Town that morning, I had put Mary's address and phone number in my pocket. I kept pulling it out every once in a while. I was trying to decide if I should spend all the money I had on me on a phone call to Mary or just go eat lunch at some restaurant in downtown Omaha.

Every once in a while another Boys Town boy would walk by. He would be by himself, just wandering around like me. I would also catch sight of some of the boys in groups. It was like we were lost in time.

Finally, on that first day in town, I decided I would go eat lunch and not bother Mary Fehrenbacker. I started looking for a restaurant that some of the Boys Town boys told me about that had a great hamburger and shake for $2.50. "If you're lucky," one kid told me on the bus into town, "you can run out the door and not pay. They never chase you. Just don't let the waitress know you're a Boys Town boy," he said proudly.

I did find the place and as I was walking in to get seated I spotted an older Boys Town boy in a booth kissing a really heavy girl with a ton of makeup on. They were hot for each other. She had on a red skirt and dark nylons. I couldn't believe anyone could be that interested in a girl who looked like that. With that sight in front of me I immediately turned and left. I went back to the pay phone I had seen downstairs in the old Brandeis department store.

I picked up the pay phone and dropped $4.50 in quarters in front of me onto the phone. My heart began to pound as the operator came on the line. She told me how much change I would have to put into the phone to make the call. I could hear each quarter go down, and with each one I wanted to talk myself out of it. I was certain Mary either would not be there or she wouldn't want to talk to me because of how strange it would seem that I would call her from Nebraska.

When I finally finished dumping the quarters into the pay phone, the operator dialed up the Fehrenbacker residence in Joliet, Illinois, 500 miles and many troublesome days away. Joliet seemed like another country and another lifetime ago.

Several rings into the call I heard, "Hello." The operator hung up and I said with a nervous voice, "Hello, Mrs. Fehrenbacker?"

"Yes," she answered and added, "Who is this?" I swallowed hard and barely got out, "Mrs. Fehrenbacker, this is Sal Di Leo. I was in Mary's class at St. Raymond's in Joliet and I am calling from Nebraska."

"Oh, my goodness, Sal! She's right here," she answered. I could hear her mother then tell Mary it was a long-distance call for her from me in Nebraska. My heart was so heavy while I waited for her to come on the phone.

"Oh, my God, Sal," Mary said with her kind voice. "How are you and I can't believe you are calling me!" she said. She was nice as usual and I quickly slipped in that I only had a little time but just wanted to say hello. I gave Mary my address and she promised to write. The call lasted only a few moments, but it was worth a year to me.

I remember being happy the rest of that first day on pass after I called her, even though my stomach was growling the rest of the day. It turned out to be a good first pass after all.

I wrote to Mary on several occasions and she wrote back. She even sent a copy of a 16mm home movie that her dad had taken of our eighth-grade graduation. I still have it. (Mary, if you are reading this, I thank you for your kindness and would like to return the tape to you.) After the first year, we lost contact.

In my mind, however, I knew I would not have a girlfriend unless she was just like Mary. I wanted a girl who was kind, intelligent, and nicely dressed.

One of the best benefits that first year was that I got to be with Mario again. Having a big brother again was the best thing that could have happened to me my first year at Boys Town. He was always looking out for me and we spent some fun times together. I really enjoyed hanging around with him and his girlfriend that year. Unfortunately, it went by much too quickly.

The following June, in 1969, Mario graduated from Boys Town. He headed to Dallas, Texas, to go to school. Again I was alone and sad. However, the summer he graduated, I made one of my best moves. I signed up to be a junior counselor at the Boys Town Camp at Lake Okaboji, Iowa.

Camp meant sunshine, water skiing, girls, and no Boys Town for the whole summer. I couldn't believe how easy it was to get the job. For some reason, most of the Boys Town kids liked to spend their summers in the Omaha area. When I found out about the position, I got permission from Mr. Keenan, our head counselor of the high school choir section, to go. I had a great summer in the sun.

Mr. Keenan and my house counselor on the high school side, Pat Render, were very exceptional Boys Town counselors. They were both very well-educated men who encouraged me to get an education, too. Dr. Jim P. Keenan was a professor at Creighton University, a judge in Omaha, and a well-respected person in the Omaha community. Pat Render was a former Boys Town boy who was just finishing his final year of law school at Creighton University under Mr. Keenan's mentorship. I was grateful to know these two men, and I am still grateful today that I had them around me after Mario left. They made the difference for me time and time again when things seemed desperate after Mario graduated.

The summer of 1969 was also an eventful one for mankind. The first man landed on the moon. I never forgot Neil Armstrong's statement as he stepped onto the moon: "That's one small step for man, one giant leap for mankind." It was a stirring moment for all of us. The world was changing very fast around me.

While I was at camp that summer, I worked out a lot and hit the weights pretty hard. I was in great physical shape by the fall of my sophomore year. When Mario came back from Texas to Omaha that Thanksgiving to see his girlfriend Vickie, who was a senior in high school, he noticed I had put on about 20 pounds of muscle. I was ready to defend myself.

I managed to get through my sophomore and junior years with as many extra-curricular activities as possible and without too much trouble. Somehow, I finally made the Concert Choir at the end of my junior year and I was told I was going to go on tour in the fall of my senior year, 1971. I couldn't wait. I had always felt the choir director never did like me after I confronted him about that horrible incident I experienced in the dorm room my first night in Building No. 3. I felt I had been passed over for that reason.

# Chapter 14
## Ann

In early June of 1971, something happened that changed everything for me for the remainder of my stay at Boys Town. Maybe even for the rest of my life.

I was out walking one warm summer evening around 6:30 p.m. The sun was still up and shining. Another fellow and I were on our way up to the field house to work out. The guy I was walking with and I were on the main road going through Boys Town, the road that the tourists usually took when they came through.

As we were walking, with our shirts off, we could hear a car coming up from behind us on the winding road. We didn't think much of it as we heard the car coming closer. People used to come in the evenings, even when the Visitor Center was closed, and drive through to look at the world-famous Boys Town. We always hated being stared at.

That particular night, instead of the car driving by, we heard it slowing down. It passed us, then stopped at the curb in front of us. It was a candy-apple red 1969 Camaro with three girls in it. Of course we noticed that right away as the driver of the car rolled down her window. We were there to help, so we immediately headed up to the car.

A blond, sort of heavyset girl was in the driver's seat, and she started asking us questions. I could see they were about our age. There was another girl in the passenger seat up front and one behind her in the back seat. As soon as I realized that the driver didn't want real directions but was trying to make conversation, I started walking on. I didn't want anything to do with her. She wasn't my type.

As I walked by the car to continue on to the field house I glanced over my shoulder into the windshield and saw that the other girl looked thin and fairly attractive. That stopped me in my tracks, and out of curiosity I walked back around the other side of the car to get a closer look at her. She had long hair, seemed nicely dressed, and looked like a nice girl. I said something to her that I don't remember, and she answered politely. I could tell she was nervous and didn't seem too comfortable being there.

Meanwhile, I couldn't see much of the girl in the back seat, let alone her face. She was hiding back there. So I chatted with the passenger while the other fellow answered a bunch of dumb questions from the driver. Just when I thought I was running out of conversation, I dropped down into a squat position to say one more thing to the girl I was talking to. It was then that I finally looked at the girl in the back.

When our eyes met, she was beet red from embarrassment and was trying to hide her face in her hands. But it was a pretty face and I liked her at first sight. At that point I made some silly statement about her hiding in the back seat. I somehow let her know I was immediately interested in her. She didn't respond too much. But when I asked what they were really doing in Boys Town at this time of the day, the girl in the passenger seat in front said it was all Sue, the driver's, idea and that the car really belonged to Ann in the back seat. When I looked again at Ann in the back seat, she smiled and turned four shades of red.

That's how I met Ann Magruder. The other girls picked up on what happened between us immediately. They knew we liked each other at our first glance. So Sue, being the master she was, quickly introduced the three of us and gave us their phone numbers. About that time the Boys Town Patrol was coming down the road and the girls pulled out. I caught one more look from Ann and we smiled at each other. She was looking over her shoulder from the back seat as they drove away. I smiled back and waved. She quickly turned forward and I could hear them laughing as they drove off. I knew right then and there I had finally found a nice girl like Mary Fehrenbacker back in Joliet. It took three long years but I knew it had been worth the wait.

After the girls left, my buddy accused me of taking his girl from him. He explained, "I had my eye on her in the back seat all along. I was just trying to get past the one in the front seat. She never gave me a chance," he finished as we ran up to the field house. I was ready to pump some iron that day.

Making phone calls at Boys Town was difficult. There were

phones in the counselors' quarters, but you almost had to be near death to use them. It was also impossible to receive calls. However, that summer another good thing had happened. Pat Render, my previous counselor, had finished law school at Creighton, gotten married, and left Boys Town. His replacement happened to be another law student from Creighton by the name of Dan Reynolds. Dan had spent time in the military and was going back to law school. He was a pretty cool guy and gave us a fresh look on life. He also let us do more normal things, such as use the phone to call girls. We liked Dan a lot.

The following night I told Dan about the girls we'd met and that I wanted to call Ann. He let me do it. When the phone rang at Ann's house, this is what I heard: "Hello. Dr. Magruder here." My throat went dry and my voice cracked when I replied. "Dr. Magruder?"

"Yes. Who am I speaking to?" he asked. I replied, "Sir, my name is Sal Di Leo and I live at Boys Town. Could I speak to Ann?"

"She's not here. Can I have her call you?" he inquired. "We're not allowed to take phone calls here, sir," I said. "Could I call back?" I pursued.

But I figured in the back of my mind that it was hopeless. It didn't seem like he cared much for me on the phone and I didn't know if she was out with someone else or what. "Well. I guess you can. Try back later this evening," he said, and hung up.

Trying to get two phone calls in one evening was tough, even with Dan. But because I was going to be a senior and was his cottage commissioner, I felt I could pull it off. I also knew how much he liked his shoes shined, being an old military man, and I put the deal in front of him: a shine for another try later. Dan submitted to my request.

That night when I called back, Ann's mother answered the phone. She was quite pleasant to me. I was encouraged. When I got Ann on the phone, Ann asked to take it upstairs in her room. Right away, I could tell she was as nervous as I was but that she was happy to hear from me. She told me she had been hoping I would call, and that's what started our relationship. She was sweet, intelligent, clean, and came from a good family. She had a car, too, and only lived about a mile from Boys Town, out in West Omaha in a newer sub-division. It worked out pretty well for us from the start.

The Magruder family was kind to me from the beginning. Ann's mom loved to cook and I loved to eat her food. Ann's little sister Martha and I became good buddies and played a lot of basketball and catch. Her brother Tom was a nice kid, too. Their family showed me what a normal family was like.

On one occasion, Dr. Magruder called Jim Keenan at Boys Town to see if I could get out more often than the designated four Saturday passes a month that the seniors were allowed. Mr. Keenan gave me extra permission when he could to encourage me to see a nice girl, but he caught pressure from other counselors about it at times.

When Mr. Keenan couldn't give me any more rope, Dr. Magruder shocked me one day with a phone call at about 3 p.m. Dan Reynolds took the call. Since it was Dr. Magruder, he allowed me to receive it.

"Sal, this is Dr. Magruder," he said. "Mr. Keenan and I just talked and I asked if you could join us for dinner a few nights a week. Keenan said with all the other kids not getting the privileges you have been given already, he couldn't pull that off. I told him I understood, but that I thought your visiting regulations are antiquated and ridiculous. However, I also told him it would be a shame if you missed a few meals here and there in the dining hall because you weren't feeling well. I think we have an understanding. Be in back of the field house at 4 o'clock. I'll spring you."

I couldn't believe my ears. But at 4 p.m., a shiny, new, red Chevy station wagon drove by the back of the field house with Dr. Magruder behind the wheel. I ran to the car and jumped in. He told me to lie down, and we laughed as we drove out the back entrance of Boys Town by the farm.

Needless to say, Dr. Magruder was a great guy, and the Magruders were wonderful people. Dr. Magruder was responsible for taking me to my first Nebraska football game and getting me enrolled in the University of Nebraska the following year. Ann was my sweetheart that senior year at Boys Town, we went to the prom, we had fun together, and she made it great. The family even took me on vacation with them to South Padre Island, Texas. The Magruders came to my high school graduation the following June, and Dr. Magruder found me a summer job at Creighton and a place to stay until I started school. I am very grateful to Ann for her love and to the Magruder family for their kindness.

Before all of that, though, I had to go on the choir tour. I didn't want to be away from Ann for 12 whole weeks. After all the anticipation and effort to make tour, I didn't want to go. But I did go, and it seemed like it took forever.

We pulled out of Boys Town in a chartered Greyhound bus in early October 1971 to finally leave for tour. As we drove out of Boys Town, I remember seeing Ann driving by and waving to me. She had waited outside the entrance to Boys Town just for that moment. "I sure love her," I thought. Ann was wonderful.

The tour was a bittersweet experience. We headed west and saw some beautiful country, from Nebraska to California and back. I remember seeing the farmers in their fields in western Nebraska, harvesting corn as the sun came up. We stopped and gave concerts, usually two a day, in all kinds of towns, like Rock Springs, Wyoming; Butte and Billings, Montana; and Wallace, Idaho, which was a beautiful old silver mining town nestled in the mountains. I'd never been outside the Midwest, and I'd never seen mountains before. We sang in towns in Washington and Oregon, and traveled down Highway 1 in California, all the way to Los Angeles. Various organizations and service clubs sponsored the tour, and we met Boys Town alumni in some of the towns.

Ann wrote to me almost every day while we were on tour. The other guys made fun of me, because everywhere we went, when we checked into the hotel and the counselor picked up the mail, I would usually have two or three letters waiting for me.

The remainder of my senior year at Boys Town went by rather quickly after the tour. Philip, Ricky, and I had managed to survive our four years at Boys Town. Philip had scholarship offers from almost every major university in the country. His offers included Harvard, MIT, Stanford, Notre Dame, Bradley, Northwestern, the University of Chicago, and the list went on.

For some odd reason, though, he picked Bradley University in Peoria, Illinois. My only guess was that he wanted to be fairly close to his mother and sister. I don't know why he didn't pick Northwestern or the University of Chicago.

Graduation Day at Boys Town was on June 4, 1972. It was a day to remember and one of the happiest days of my life. For me, it was the end of a long sentence.

After our graduation ceremony, I went over to Ricky Barker to say to goodbye. Ricky's older brother, I believe, as well as his mother, sister, and other family members, had come in from Illinois to see him. I wished him well. I have never heard from him since. I did hear he went into the military a few years later from another Boys Town graduate.

I found Philip to say goodbye and asked where he was headed since he did not have family at graduation. He said he was going to hitchhike to Omaha and hang out there for a few days. We were 18 years old, and we had been through a lot together. I told him I was going home with the Magruders for a few days and then I would be staying in the dorms at Creighton University in downtown Omaha for the rest of the summer. I told him I had a job (which Dr. Magruder got me) painting the dormitories and they had offered me $1.50 an hour, a meal ticket, and a free room. I told him if he couldn't find a place to stay he could stay with me for a few days.

Two nights after our graduation, I got a knock on the door about 8 o'clock in the evening. It was Philip. He ended up staying all summer. He managed to talk the priest at Creighton into renting him a room on the same floor as me in Kiewit Hall for almost nothing. He got a job somewhere off campus and we palled around all summer.

During that summer I also saw Ann a great deal and ate poor Mrs. Magruder out of house and home. I was free at last! What still sticks in my mind is how I couldn't get over how every night that summer I could stay out late and go wherever I wanted without asking permission from anyone. Philip and I walked around many nights until late talking about so many things.

Many times our conversations were about our years in institutions. For the first time in our lives, no one told us it was time for bed or that we were in trouble for not being back for check-in. It was a fantasy for me. That was the best summer of my life for a long time. I finally felt I was in charge of my own life and no one else would interfere and tell me what to do. It was truly a blissful summer.

By late August of 1972, Philip and I knew it was time to move on. He had his plans and I had mine. He was going to hitchhike to Peoria and I was going to Lincoln for school. Somehow, I didn't worry about Philip getting to Illinois. Maybe I never gave it a second thought. Maybe I should have. I guess I was only thinking of myself and didn't consider Philip's future. He seemed ready at that time and was off in his own world. I feel we both somehow understood that to survive on our own neither of us could hold each other back. It was the unspoken rule for us at the time. I said goodbye, shook his hand, and we looked each other in the eye as men. We had fought the war together and we had won.

# Chapter 15
## Life begins at the University of Nebraska

The Magruder family came over to Creighton to pick up all my earthly belongings (which consisted of everything in my trunk) and me, and we headed to Lincoln, Nebraska, to check in to school. Ann and I were heading off to college together.

We were both pretty excited that day, but Ann was also scared and sad about leaving home. Dr. and Mrs. Magruder, Ann, Tom, Martha, and I went in the red station wagon, loaded with my stuff. They were dropping me off a day early, and Ann was coming down the next day.

Beside my trunk, two brand-new 10-speed bikes were dismantled in the back. One was for me and one for Ann. Dr. Magruder said I needed a bike to get around the big campus in Lincoln, so he bought me one as a graduation present. He was kind to do that, especially since I did not have a car.

When we arrived at Harper Hall, which was the men's dorm, just across the courtyard from Smith Hall, which was where Ann was going to stay, the reality that I was really going to college and could maybe be somebody someday began to sink in. I was awed by the campus and all of its possibilities. It was like I had finally been lifted out of the dungeon I was born into.

As soon as they got me settled in, Dr. Magruder opened my window on the fifth floor and noticed a train track about 50 yards behind the dorm. "Sal. Do you like the sound of trains?" he asked. "I don't know. I guess I never thought of it before," I replied. "Well, you'll know soon if you do," he said with a grin.

I found out what he meant that night when a train came through three times and blew its horn as loud and long as it could. As the year progressed, the guys in the dorm discussed the theory that it was the same bastard who drove that train every night and his only lot in life was to piss off every guy in Harper Hall. One of our fellow students even went so far as to speculate that it might have been a former Oklahoma football player who was driving that train because he was too dumb to get a real job. We decided a train derailment was definitely a possibility that year.

I had managed to get into the dorm a day ahead of everyone else because of Dr. Magruder's arrangement. The only other people in the dorm that first night were the Student Assistants (SAs). SAs were the students who were in charge of attempting to hold the place together during the school year.

Each floor in the dorm had at least one SA. Mark Johnson from Omaha was ours and he was a nice kid. After Ann and the Magruders left to go back to Omaha, it was about noon on Saturday. Mark told me where I could get something to eat. Downtown Lincoln was walking distance, he said.

I did just that. I walked all over campus and downtown until 11 o'clock. It was a mystical night. I was so excited to be in Lincoln and a student at the University of Nebraska. I remember looking out my window that first night and feeling so excited that I had life by the big toe.

When Ann and her family came back the next day, they found me upstairs in my room. I went over to help her move into Smith Hall. By this time cars, kids, and families were everywhere. You could feel the buzz in the air. It was a beautiful, warm, sunny day in Lincoln and there was a lot of excitement everywhere you looked.

Poor Ann had puffy eyes though. I could tell she had been crying. She was a sensitive girl and she had never been away from home. I assured her I would be there with her. Besides, she had a car and was only an hour, at most, away from home. She still cried when her parents left. Her mom cried, too.

Our first night together in Lincoln was just great, though. As we started exploring the campus together she got excited and the homesick feeling wore off. We found the art gallery on campus and walked by some of the landmarks we had heard about. She'd been on campus many times with her family, who were great Nebraska fans, so she knew where to go. It was fun.

We walked downtown and went out for pizza. Then we walked around by the fountain by the Student Union and just enjoyed the warm summer night air. College kids were everywhere. There was a buzz in the air. We had fun and quickly realized how much freedom this whole college life was going to bring.

On Monday, the first day of classes, it was time to jump out of bed and get ready to go.

The cafeteria was in the middle of the Harper, Schram, and Smith dorm complex, separating the men's dorm from Smith Hall, where the women stayed. I was to meet Ann and her roommate for breakfast on the first day of class.

I hit the showers early and got ready to go. Real college life was about to begin for me. I was nervous and a little excited. The dorm was buzzing. Guys were scrambling everywhere- to the showers, to their rooms, or wherever.

I hooked up that morning with the only person on the fifth floor in Harper Hall that I knew before I came to Lincoln, a guy by the name of Sam Peery. I met Sam in high school through Ann Magruder at one of her high school's basketball games in Omaha. Sam dated a sweet little gal by the name of Barb, Ann's best friend in high school and was her roommate in Smith Hall that first year at Nebraska.

A guy whom I will call "Meat Ball," for the sake of anonymity, and who introduced himself to everyone on the floor as the "Social Chairman of Harper Five" the first day of move-in, was out in the hall. As Sam and I headed down the hall, Meat Ball was hanging out his door quietly observing all the commotion. He had informed us all the first day that anything in the line of crucial goods, such as beer, girls, or whatever, could be sufficiently supplied by him for just a meager fee. " I am here for you boys!" he'd exclaimed the first night in the dorm.

Meat Ball hung his wobbly head out the door of his room that morning, with his long thinning hair draping down, with a beer in his hand, a cigarette blazing, smelling of the Herb's he had smoked the night before. He studied Sam and me intently as we passed by his door on our way to breakfast.

"You guys going to eat?" he mumbled. "Yeah. Want to go?" Sam asked politely.

"No! I just wanted to see who was making all the damn racket out here so early in the morning. How the hell is a guy supposed to get any sleep around here?" Meat Ball slurred in his most polite manner. With that, our newly self-appointed Social Chairman stumbled back into his room and shoved the door shut with his foot to begin his first day of classes.

Just then we heard a voice behind us say, "Hey, we'll join you guys!" As Sam and I turned around, a short, chubby guy with a nice smile and round, wire-rimmed glasses, with a white pin striped shirt and suspenders came from around the corner with his hand out. His hair was parted and slicked down the middle to just above his ears, and he looked like he had just gotten off a train in the Old West.

The little fella grabbed Sam's hand and shook it as he introduced himself. "Ben Shomshor's the name. From Fremont Nebraska!" he exclaimed with a pleasant and intelligent-sounding voice. "And this is my roommate and best friend, Jim Steckelberg, from Fremont, Nebraska, as well!"

I caught the twinkle in Sam's eye as he shook Ben's hand and grinned. We both immediately liked this well-mannered little guy and his friend. They were to become the floor connoisseurs of good food, wine (which none of us beer-drinking Cornhusker fools had ever brought to our sorry lips before), and good literature. Ben later introduced the floor to J.R.R. Tolkien and started the Tolkien Club, which required having a pipe in your hand before you were allowed into their room. Ben and Jim's room was a trip into another dimension for the rest of us average guys. With their eclectic mix of unusual furniture, a full-sized refrigerator, and sophisticated study areas for each of them, one could only imagine where these guys managed to come up with all the paraphernalia they had stuffed into 10 x 14 foot dorm room. Their room gave us all the impression that just maybe there was hope that somebody in this worthless bunch of Harper Five thugs had actually come to college with the honorable intention of really getting an education. I think we all secretly admired them for it. They were our poindexters.

"Join us you can, Ben Shomshor and Jim Steckelberg from Fremont," Sam said. "The name is Sam Peery from Omaha, and this is my friend, Sal Di Leo, also from Omaha." With that, a great friendship began as the four of us piled into an already over stuffed elevator on its way down from the tenth floor.

As the four of us crossed the center courtyard and headed toward the cafeteria, the bright early sunshine of late summer broke over Schram Hall and lit the front entrance of the cafeteria. The morning dew on the grassy courtyard reflected the light and seemed to illuminate the new journey that was begging that morning in my life. I felt as if it was almost magical, almost surreal, the way the building was lit, and the excitement in my mind.

As we entered the cafeteria, I spotted Ann and Barb at the head of the line and called to them to get us a table by the windows. "We'll meet you in there," I yelled.

Once we were in the cafeteria and in line to grab our trays, it hit me. I found myself almost in a trance as I lost myself in that moment of tranquility. "Ah," I sighed, with a smile on my face. "What," Ben asked as he impatiently waited to get to the food line.

Without losing my gaze off into nowhere, I asked in a quiet and happy voice, "Do you smell that?"

"Yeah," Ben responded with satisfaction as he found himself wandering off to a happy place in the back of his mind. "Hash Browns!" he replied.

"No, not that, you idiot," I answered, coming back to reality.

"Bacon?" Ben asked desperately, trying to prove his worth to his newly found college chums.

"Girls!", I proclaimed. "I can smell the wonderful fragrance of girls," I said with utter satisfaction.

"Ben, Jim, and Sam looked at each other with surprised and perplexed faces and my mind drifted off again, delighted at how wonderful it was to be in college and away from locked doors, as well as the smell of jock straps and Boys Town boys. "God, I am going to love this place," I said as loud as I could, scurrying to catch up with the other guys.

By this time, Ben was already piling on as much bacon and hash browns as he could convince the cafeteria help to give him. "Yeah," I'm going to love this place, too," he confirmed.

I guess even old Meat Ball must have decided that day he was going to love the college life as well. His world of sleeping late and partying all night with no responsibility must have been all one could hope for in his carefully planned education at the University Of Nebraska. As the semester went along, Meat Balls's incredible 0.0 grade point average held steady, proving to any silent nay-sayer on Harper Five that our friend truly was the right man for the job of "Social Chairman". Unfortunately, even legendary Meat Ball was subject to life's cruel reminders of reality. The day Meat Ball's first semester grades hit home his dad drove down from Omaha to discuss it personally with his beloved son. It must have been around 2:30 in the afternoon, just about Meat Ball's time to wake up and start his day. It was to be the last time any of us on Harper Five ever saw our "Social Chairman" again. If my memory serves me well, he was being dragged down the hall by the ear, screaming "Dad, what about my stuff?"

Jim Steckleberg and Ben Shomsher, however, lived up to their billing as smart kids. Jim went on to make the Dean's list and the Honors Program. He even became a Rhodes Scholar, went off to study in England, finally went on to medical school at the Mayo Clinic in Rochester, Minnesota. Ben ended up getting exceptional grades as well, but decided his creative talents were not to be wasted. The last I heard, he had become a master chef at some fancy restaurant out East.

Despite all the new distractions, commotion and excitement that campus life offered me, my freshman classes went well. My first class set the pace for me. It was a literature teacher named Clyde Berkholder. I walked in that first day and he was sitting on top of his desk, just talking to a couple of kids. He gave us our syllabus and told us we didn't have to show up for class if we didn't want to, and it was up to us if we wanted to learn. I was used to the regimented Boys Town classes. I thought he was such a cool guy, I really enjoyed his class.

So I could get by, I had to work part time during the semester to pay for school. I did all I could to make ends meet and I had some grants and loans, and I got a job in the microbiology lab. I really like the old guy who ran the lab. He hired me during his last year before his retirement after 30-some years in the lab. I went in the first day of school and asked him if he needed any help. He said he had a full crew but he took a liking to me. I told him I didn't have any way to pay for school if I didn't get a job, and so he created one for me because someone had done the same for him back during the depression when he needed a break to go to school. He really turned out to be a great old friend. We swapped a lot stories about our youth and always wanting to make it in life when we were kids. I owe the old guy a lot. When he retired the next spring I went to his retirement party and he was pretty teary eyed.

I fell in love with Nebraska football, made a lot of friends, and enjoyed every minute of it. There is something to be said about the whole college experience that is beyond the books that you carry all through your life. It is a chance I think to grow and see the big picture in life and still be a kid for a few more precious years of your youth. It was great and I felt right at home in college my freshman year and that I was going somewhere finally with my life.

# Chapter 16
## Goodbye Ann

I was sad about the first year of college ending, although I loved summer in general. I would miss all my friends until school started back.

Worse than school being out for the summer was that after our freshman year, Ann and I began to grow apart. She had decided she was in need of a little space from me and that she needed to breathe. She felt like we were too young to get serious. After all, I was her first boyfriend and she needed to find out what it was like to date other guys, for a while at least.

I couldn't understand, though, and did not make it easy for her. She told me at the end of the school year. I took it very hard. I couldn't sleep or think of anything for about the first week when school was out. I had gotten my job back at Creighton and was living at the dorm again. But I didn't have Ann or her family to visit with at night or on the weekends and that made everything very different. It was a lonely time for me. I was heartbroken.

My brother Mario was living at that time in southern California. He had moved there from Texas about a year earlier. Our brothers Ross and Chuck were living in California, too. After not having Ann in my life, I needed someone to talk to. Who else was there to lean on but Mario? So I called him one night and told him I was having a rough time with the breakup. He had met Ann and thought highly of her, too. But most importantly, after his freshman year in college, his old girlfriend Vickie had made the same decision, and he also took it hard. He said what carried him through were his crazy Texas buddies and several thousand longneck beers.

"Get your butt out here to California for the summer," he said. "There are beaches, girls, and beer everywhere," he added. "You'll be all right and get over Ann," he reassured me. Mario sent me the airline ticket and I headed out to California.

That summer in California was a long one, though. I stayed at Mario's apartment in Alhambra, a suburb of Los Angeles. Although I was supposed to be helping Mario with a little business he had building pedestal-style chess tables, I did more moping than working. Mario covered for me that summer with almost everything. I really owed him. All summer, however, no matter what girl I saw or what we did, I thought of Ann. I couldn't wait for school to start back up again. I hoped Ann would have had enough of the dating around thing when I got back and everything would be the same again. I was also looking forward to getting back to school with my friends. Ann, however, didn't feel the same way I did, and we never did put it back together.

# Chapter 17
## A ghost from the past

Sam Peery and I had decided early in the spring of our freshman year that we would be roommates our sophomore year at Nebraska. We had become good friends while dating Ann and Barb, who were roommates our freshman year. We did a lot of double dating and got to know each other pretty well. We thought we would be good roommates.

About the second day I was back at school, Sam and I heard a knock on our dorm room door. When I opened it, I was shocked to see who was there. It was Philip Belcher. I hadn't seen him since we'd said goodbye at Creighton just before school started a year earlier.

I was taken aback by him unexpectedly being there. But, most importantly, I was surprised by the way he looked. I thought he looked terrible. He had unkempt long hair, with a scrawny-looking excuse for a beard. He had on a dirty, worn, green sweatshirt, a ragged pair of torn, dirty, bell-bottom jeans, and a backpack. That was the extent of his gear, and he smelled bad.

My first reaction when I saw Philip was not to be happy but shocked. I asked with surprise and disgust, "Philip, what are you doing here and why aren't you back at school?"

"I'm dropping out," he said without any further explanation. "I think I'll just bum for a year and see the country," he said. "Then maybe go back," he added. Finally, after I looked at him for a while with a dumbfounded expression on my face, he asked, "Can I crash here for a few days?"

I hesitantly let Philip into the room and introduced him to Sam. I could see Sam was a bit taken aback by his appearance, too, but he was nice to him and shook his hand. Sam said Philip was welcome to crash on the floor for a few days.

I was always ashamed of being from Boys Town, and when I graduated from that place I didn't want anyone to know I was from there. Sam knew, but he knew my feelings about the place and he knew not to tell anyone. He always respected that and kept my secret.

71

Right after I let Philip into the room, I told him not to mention to anyone I went to Boys Town. He acknowledged me in his own way, but I could tell he was studying me. "I want to go on with my life Philip. I am going places here and Boys Town is a bad memory. I am somebody here."

Philip could also tell I was not comfortable with the way he looked and I tried to let him know that. I thought to myself, "With the mind he has, maybe reality has bored him. Maybe he is disenchanted with all the bullshit." His mind was somehow above all of us and maybe he couldn't buy into the system like I had. My only goal was to break the chain I had been born into so my children would not suffer like I had. I never forgot the promise I made to myself in the Orphanage when I was alone in that bed when I first got there. I did not want my children to ever be alone or suffer. I somehow understood it would be a lifelong commitment. My education was too important for me to walk away from it. I wanted that degree, at whatever cost. I thought that was the answer.

I took Philip to the cafeteria with me and bought him dinner that night. I wasn't too friendly with him. A lot of kids sort of looked at him and I knew they were wondering about him. He could feel how uncomfortable I was. That night, he went to sleep on the floor. Sometime in the night, however, he slipped away. I have never heard from him again.

When Sam and I realized Philip had left, I was ashamed of myself deep down for being such a phony. I wondered what would happen to him. I feared he would get into big-time drugs and fall apart. I hoped not and hoped he would get back to school. At that time in my life he was my oldest friend, and we had gone through a lot together over the 11 years we had known each other. "What a waste if he ends up in the gutter," I thought. Philip was my hope for all of us orphans at the Guardian Angel Home, the one person who I thought had the best chance of really making it. Now he was gone and I somehow felt sorry for him like I did the day I punched him in the eye early on in the orphanage. He looked so pathetic in my mind like he did back then. I felt I had let him down.

# Chapter 18
## Without warning

During the course of my stay at Nebraska, after Ann and I broke up, I began to date a gal named Rusty Goins from Grand Island, Nebraska, who was a friend of Ann's and that lived on her floor in Smith Hall. We tried to date for awhile but it didn't work out.

Rusty's family however took a liking to me and sort of adopted me as their college kid who had no place to call home. Russell and Peggy Goins decided to give me a family again and they sort of took over where Ann Magruder's family had left off.

I got a letter one day from Peggy that had $20.00 in it with a note that said, "Just because you two broke up, we still love you. Take the Continental Trailways bus out to Grand Island and we'll pick you up. Our home is your home."

Grand Island was about 100 miles west of Lincoln and was out in the heart of the Nebraska prairie lands along the great Platt river. I took the bus out the next Saturday and there they were, two kind older folks from the Midwest who wanted to share their family with a kid with no home, waiting for me. It was really nice and I soon felt at home with these simple and kind people. They had horses and lived out of town with dogs, cats, etc. It was so peaceful that I would go out there at least once a month. Since they didn't have a son they soon referred to me as "our boy" to their family and friends. Thus began a wonderful life-long friendship that has lasted to this day. I had a place to call home again and I was still in college. Things really seemed to be going my way again.

Life, however, always seems to have a way of reminding us that every day is a gift and that we need to be grateful for each day. With little warning things can change forever. This was the case in the middle of the spring semester in 1974 during my sophomore year.

I will never forget that morning in early March when Sam got in a terrible car accident that took the life of two of our friends who were in the car with him. Sam was in a coma and in intensive care when my friends finally caught up with me to tell me the news.

When I got to the hospital I remember the horrible feeling of not knowing what to do or say. I found Sam's dad holding up the crying father of Sam's best friend in high school, whose son had just been pronounced dead. They looked so sad and I just couldn't understand what they must have been feeling like. I wanted to put my arms around both of them and tell them how sorry I felt but I just didn't know if I should. My mind was racing with so many emotions. I thought also at how bad I had always wanted a dad, when I was a kid in the orphanage. Now to see these two who loved their kids with their hearts being ripped out of them was almost more than I could handle. Even though they were both in their early 50's, they looked so old in that frozen moment in time. They looked so beaten down. I am sure the father of that young man who lost his life that night would rather have had his life taken in his son's place. "What a loss. What for?" I painfully and angrily thought while I looked on in numbness.

Sam's friend Rick was a great young man who had come down from Omaha with us to go to Nebraska in 1972. He was the driver of the car that had just left a kegger party outside of the city limits of Lincoln and he somehow misjudged the distance of a semi truck that hit them broadside at 60 miles an hour. Rick and a sweet young lady named Kathy died that lonely night on the side of a cold dark highway out in the endless prairie of Nebraska. Also died that night was my fantasy world of "no pain or harm in college" that I had surrounded myself with at the University Of Nebraska to forget about Boys Town and being in the orphanage.

Sam stayed in a coma for quite some time and when he finally did come out of it, he was in for a long rehabilitation. All of us did everything we could to help him put his life back together. I don't believe he ever was the same when he came back to school the following fall. We were still good friends, however, I choose to move to a different dorm complex and start anew in the Fall of 1974. I thought I needed to keep moving so I could get through school and get on with my goal of having a better life some day.

# Chapter 19
## The "Hebes"

An opportunity arose for me to become a Student Assistant (SA) at the Able-Sandoz student residence halls. This was a very large dormitory complex across the campus. As an SA I would receive free room and board. I needed the money. All I had to do was keep the place in order on the 8th floor of Able Hall. "Piece of Cake!" I remember thinking.

I don't believe anyone could have prepared me for the "Hebes". It was the nickname that the last poor SA had dubbed to the rowdiest group of residents to have ever resided in the 20 year old dorm complex.

"What's a 'Hebe'?" I asked the dorm director during my SA orientation that fall, just before the students arrived. "Oh. It's just a name given to the guys on your floor.

They're really a great bunch once you get to know them. You have the charisma it will take to do just fine with this group of young men, the majority of which are from the friendly little south-central community of Hebron, Nebraska", he soft-sold me with.

When the so called "great bunch" showed up that first day of move-in, two things were clear. They were all very big and they didn't like SA's. "Wasn't Hebron a bad place in the Old Testament?" I tried to remember when they kept getting off the elevator. When I stuck my hand out to introduce myself to them with enthusiasm, I almost always got the "you're our new SA?" and was usually accompanied with loud bursts of heavy belly laughter.

Needless to say, the first month on the job I earned ever last mouth full of cafeteria food I ate. That lumpy old bed they gave me turned out to be my last resort to hide under if they busted the door down and wanted to kill me.

After multiple toilets being blown off the walls, elevator breakages, urinations in the halls, and outright hell raising every night when they came home from the bars, I had to make a clear choice. "Do I leave in the middle of the night or in broad day light like a man?" I found myself struggling with this time and time again during that first month as an SA on Able 8.

Strangely enough, the "Hebes" actually had one thing in common that surprised me. It turned out to be their Achilles tendon. Every night they would come up after dinner and study. You could walk the hall from just after dinner until around 9:30 PM and think "All is Quiet on the Western Front." They really did study. Then however, it would happen. It was like dominos on a roll as you could hear the books start to slam shut, starting at far end of the hall and working its' way down toward my door at the end. "Hey, hey, hey!" one "Hebe" would shout as they began to pile out into the hall and gather in a moving mob toward the elevators and stairwells on their way to the bars.

One particular night, just before I had given up all hope of saving the dorm floor from total destruction, they came home from the bars, blew up the toilets again, and I finally lost it. I called the police and had several of them arrested. I will never forget the look on their faces when they were being dragged off to the Lincoln Jail looking at me over their shoulders. "I am going to die!" I somberly said to myself.

The next day, which I seem to think was a Saturday, the Hebron fathers rode into to town to get their boys out of jail. I had caught wind of this from one of the kids who had gotten away the night before as he talked over the toilet stall to another "Hebe". "Unit is dead," he said with satisfaction. "Yup," the other echoed from his toilet as he read the paper. "Unit," was the nick name they gave me. On the first day one of them pegged me as the "Little Unit." "Unit," stuck.

If ever there was proof there was a God to me in those days, I witnessed it first hand that day. About mid-afternoon, as I hid out in my room, while I was role playing in my mind my exit strategy in the case of all out bedlam, I received a knock at my door. As I slowly opened the door and peeked out, I saw two of the three guys who had been arrested the night before outside my door. Before I could faint, I heard the first one say, "Our dad said to say we are sorry. So we are sorry!" Apparently, they got a good licking or chewing out from their hard working small town dads about going to jail. For the rest of the year, things never really were out of control again. As a matter of fact, I truly liked those guys more and more as the year went on. We all became friends as it turned out.

I learned years later that one of the two guys who got arrested turned out to be a prominent attorney in Lincoln and his brother, who was arrested with him, became a very successful business man. As a matter of fact, a good many of the "Hebes" turned out to become doctors, dentists, research scientists, and many other professions. Who would have guessed?

During college, I also spent three summers as a camp counselor at Camp Winaukee in New Hampshire. My friend Dan Higgins, a swimmer at Nebraska, had worked there the year before and knew the director. He helped me write a letter and I ended up being hired to start a track program at the camp. Dan and I packed up my canary-yellow Super Beetle with the University of Nebraska sticker in the back and left Lincoln on May 12 with $75 between us. Gas was 26 cents a gallon. We finally got to camp a month later with a dollar and a quarter left, which we spent on breakfast at a diner in a little town outside camp. I made some of the best friends I've ever had, and I really learned a lot about myself. The campers were mostly wealthy kids from the New York City area, and for some reason, the junior-high kids I worked with really locked on to me.

The remainder of my time at the University of Nebraska was extremely happy. I got decent grades, made a lot of friends, and finally got my degree.

I was very grateful to the University of Nebraska, my alma mater, for all the help I got from the teachers and staff, who had given me so much by the time I was finished there. I was very proud to be a graduate of the University of Nebraska.

On my graduation day in Lincoln in 1977, however, I didn't attend the graduation ceremony because I couldn't afford the cap and gown and other costs. Instead, I helped set up a circus that had come to town for $2.50 an hour.

I didn't have the money that day to even buy lunch because the cafeteria was closed. But I was very proud of myself that day. I felt great inside. I was the first Di Leo to graduate from college out of the 12 of us kids in my family. It was one of my greatest days ever.

# Chapter 20
## Thrown out of the nest

Leaving the University of Nebraska was tough for me. I understood why some people become professional students. It was almost a perfect fantasy world for young people. But it was time to move on. I had no choice.

I was not sure of where I was going. I found myself in a panic and began to get angry again. It seems like I fell apart at this time and felt powerless like I did back in Boys Town. I did not want to leave the womb of college. I did not have the support my friends all did. They had family to fall back on and places to go. Some were going on to dental school, law school, graduate school, or just good jobs. I was broke and felt alone again. Even though I had the Goins family behind me as friends, I knew I was on my own. I couldn't expect much more out of them than a place to go home to for a weekend visit. I was very appreciative to have that, though.

So, my early 20s after college were not very happy for me. I took a job as a teacher in Fremont, Nebraska, teaching fourth grade. Though I enjoyed teaching and enjoyed the kids, the money just wasn't there. I made $7,000 that year and could hardly pay the rent, let alone take a girl out or have any money to even get new clothes. As a matter of fact, I usually ran out of money before the end of the month and on occasion didn't have anything to eat.

One day, about two days before payday, I was really hungry. That afternoon I received a letter by surprise from Peggy and Russell. Enclosed with a letter of support was a brand new $10 bill. I almost cried with joy. It meant a lot to me. Peggy and Russell were truly considerate people. With their help I made it through that first year out of college.

The following summer, just before school was out, I gave my notice to the Fremont Schools that I was resigning. I surprised the superintendent. She recruited me and she was very disappointed. I thought highly of her and appreciated her hiring me. I just knew teaching wasn't going to take me where I wanted to go. "Besides," I thought, "I've got a degree and that's worth something."

After I cleaned out my stuff at Clarkson Elementary School, I packed my yellow 1971 Volkswagen Super Beetle and went back to camp in New England to be a camp counselor again. I had worked at camp as a counselor for the previous three summers and made great friends from all over the country, and I was able to save some money. "I can be a college kid again until I figure out what I am going to do with my life," I told Peggy and Russell Goins after I dropped what little stuff I had off at their home in Grand Island, Nebraska.

It was great to be back again at Camp Winaukee. The great counselor friends from all over were up there and it was fun. During the course of that summer, I decided I had it in me to become a businessman. I was going to try and get a job as a salesman or something when I got back to Nebraska. It was the summer of 1978.

Not long after I got back from camp I found an assistant manager's job at a TV rental store in Omaha. This move proved to be a lucrative one for me. Within six months I was promoted to store manager and I was making over $2,500 a month. That was more than three times my teaching salary.

I bought a new sports car and moved into a great place to live. After a year I was promoted to district manager and was making over $3,000 a month. I felt like I was going straight to the top.

It was then that I began to change. I did not have a steady girlfriend at the time so I spent more and more time at the bars. I began drinking a lot more and found myself looking for wild women instead of the nice girls I used to date. I also began using marijuana on occasion and stopped going to church.

Life just had a different meaning for me during the time I was 22 to 25 years old. I was on a quest to prove to the world that I had made it: becoming wealthy would prove it. Money was all I cared about.

I soon found myself alone. My old friends from college started avoiding me because they could see the change. Thank goodness for Peggy and Russell Goins, who stayed with me during this time in my life and always reminded me I could come home to Grand Island, Nebraska. Going to their home always helped me get back on track.

Since I was not interested in nice girls at the time, on more than one occasion I brought a wild-looking girl home with me to Grand Island. Peggy and Russell would make her feel at home, but I could tell they didn't approve of her. I'm not sure how or why they stayed with me during those tumultuous years, but they did. They must have had hope I would get through it. It seemed like a long period of time for me, though. I was lonely inside, and unhappy, but I didn't care about anything but making money because it would take the feeling of being powerless away from me, I thought.

"You need to meet a nice girl who will help you settle down," Peggy told me one day after I brought another sleazy one home with me. "She is nice to me," I said with a smart-aleck reply. "You know what I mean," Peggy replied as her eyes rolled.

# Chapter 21
## Another nice girl

I had always been lucky when it came to women. I don't mean "lucky" as in getting them into bed easily. I mean, I had managed to find good women—maybe because I was attracted to them. The best advice I ever got from anyone about a relationship with a woman came from old Mr. Keenan at Boys Town when he saw I was dating Ann Magruder.

"Sal, take care of that girl," he said as he stuck $5 in my hand one Saturday morning while I was getting on the bus to go on pass. "If you learn to respect women you will find a good one someday. There's nothing better in life than a good marriage. But," the old Irish Catholic went on to say, "there is nothing worse than a bad woman. She will destroy your life. So, when you get a good one, take care of her."

I knew Mr. Keenan was right. I had known it ever since I was in the orphanage. I wanted to rise above the situation I was born into. Somehow, in the back of my mind, I always knew I could break the chain I was born into if I could find a good woman to be my wife and raise my children. I don't know how I knew that, but I just did.

On the day Mr. Keenan gave me that advice back at Boys Town, I was extra nice to Ann and was glad she was my girlfriend. Somehow, after I left the university, during my early 20s, I got off track on that. I guess I didn't want to settle down yet.

On my day off from work one day, when I was about 24, I went over to play tennis on the courts near the Mutual of Omaha area. I liked that old part of Omaha. It had quaint old apartment buildings and interesting houses. It wasn't far from Creighton University or downtown Omaha. It was where the young professionals lived and hung around. I liked interacting with them because it made me feel like I was one of them. A lot of medical students from Creighton or young executives from Mutual of Omaha lived and hung around there and played tennis on these courts.

At that time, I wasn't in the best physical shape and I was

pasty white from a lack of sun from working on weekends in the stores. It was August. However, I had my white tennis shorts and a white tennis shirt on. I thought I looked pretty cool. As I drove up to the tennis courts, I noticed right away a cute little gal over at the wall in a little short tennis skirt, hitting against the wall by herself. She had curly brown hair and looked nice. She also looked a little bit older than me. I liked that.

As I approached her, she hit a ball that went behind her and I retrieved it. "Would you like to hit with me for a little while?" I asked in my fake confident voice. "OK" she said with some level of uncertainty. I could tell she was sizing me up and didn't like what she saw.

When we went over to the courts and began hitting, she immediately commenced kicking my butt on the tennis court for about an hour. She could tell I dressed the part (barely) but couldn't play tennis worth a darn. Soon, she made it clear she needed to go.

"Say," I said, "Would you like to go out for a beer or something?" I asked. "No," she said with irritation in her voice.

"Why not?" I boldly asked. "Because you're not my type," she said with no mercy.

"Well then, what's your name?" I asked just so I could get something out of her and so she wouldn't leave my ego completely deflated. "My name is Beth. Goodbye," she said as she climbed into her new Volkswagen Rabbit. When she drove off, I thought, "What a snob."

I ran into Beth off and on over the next few years and it was always short and uncomfortable for us. We were not meant to be. She just didn't have time for me. She made it clear I wasn't her type.

On one occasion, however, several years after we first met, I managed to get her phone number and address. "Is it OK if I call you for a drink sometime?" I asked when we ran into each other at the Fine Arts Dance performance at the Orpheum Theater in Omaha. I think she was surprised to see me there. I also thought that maybe I had made an impression on her that night. "Hey, if this loser is at a theater production," I thought she might be thinking, "maybe he is worth taking a risk on to go out for a harmless drink some night."

About two weeks later, on a Saturday afternoon, I decided to pop in on her to see what she was doing. I didn't call first. I just drove over with the thought that she would be glad to see me and that we would finally go out. Hey, it was Saturday and I was sure she'd jump on it.

When I got to her door at the old apartment building where she lived (a very interesting and delightful building), an older man came to the door. "Hello," he said to me, "Can I help you?" He was a well-dressed, distinguished-looking man in his 60s.

"Um," I choked out, "Is this Beth's apartment?"

"Yes. Would you like to speak to her? I'm her father from Minnesota. Doctor Kirby's my name," he said.

Boy, was I uncomfortable. "Yes, sir," I replied. He turned and said to Beth, "Bethie, there's a young man at the door to see you." I could hear Beth in the other room talking to another person. "Ask who it is, Dad," she yelled back. "What is your name, young man?" he asked. At this time I was really uncomfortable. "My name is Sal," I said almost in a panic. His face got a bit puzzled as he wheeled around and said, "His name is Sal." "Tell him to go away, Dad. He didn't call and make an appointment." Before old Dr. Kirby could give me the news, I cut him short, did an about-face, and headed down the three flights of stairs. "What a snob. She did it to me again," I thought.

About a year later I ran into Beth again. This time, it was at the indoor track at Creighton. I did a lot of jogging in those days and was quite competitive in running middle distance races. As a matter of fact, I was one of the better racers in the Omaha area and placed well in most 5K and 10K races.

That particular Saturday afternoon in January I took a younger girl whom I really didn't like much with me to the track. But I wanted a date that night. I figured if we ran together, that maybe she would go out with me later that night. She was a pretty good runner and I had met her at one of the races a few months earlier.

When the girl and I began jogging and talking, I remember

thinking what an airhead she was.

About the third lap, I noticed Beth in there jogging also, rather slowly. I picked up my pace and left the other girl behind. As I ran past Beth (rather quickly, to impress her) I said "Hey." Beth said, "Hi," back.

About that time, the girl who I came with asked me to slow down. I know Beth heard her. But I picked up the pace and left her behind. About a mile later, I found Beth walking so I stopped and started talking with her. By then, the other girl had left out of frustration.

"What are you doing here?" I asked Beth. "I work for the Boys Town Institute in Audiology and we get to use this facility since our department is a part of Creighton University," she said. Somehow, we sort of connected that day and she asked me about the other girl. I said I didn't know what happened to her. "She must have left," I said. I also managed to get Beth's phone number again. I could tell she was more receptive to me that day, for some unknown reason.

The next day, remembering the last time I showed up without an appointment, I called her first and asked her out to dinner. She had told me it was her birthday the day before. I was surprised that she accepted. We went to Salvatore's for dinner in Omaha. It was a fairly decent restaurant. She was dressed very well and I showed up in my polyester suit, with an extra-wide tie, and platform shoes. She wasn't too impressed.

A couple of weeks later, I saved grace with Beth when I asked her out again. This time, she reluctantly agreed. I asked her if she wanted to go hiking in a place called Wabonsi State Park. It was in the corner of Nebraska, Iowa, and Missouri. "On the top of the highest hill you can see three states from one point," I told her to impress her. She wasn't too amused, but she accepted.

Instead of showing up in my K-Mart specials like I did on our first dinner date, I showed up in a pair of jeans, hiking boots, a decent sweater, and my leather coat. She opened the door of her apartment and looked rather surprised at me. "I think she's not going to throw me out this time," I thought. She was dressed in designer jeans and expensive leather shoes, and had a picnic basket loaded with food and wine. We had a great day. We laughed and we ended up kissing a lot. I think she fell for me that day. It was an answer to my prayers.

Beth and I became very close very quickly from that day on. Somehow we had both changed since when we had first met on the tennis court more than years earlier. We had both come closer to the middle. She turned out to be a sweet and wonderful friend very soon. Unbelievably, we were married ten months later. I was 27 and Beth was 30.

Our wedding, in Rochester, Minnesota, was a great time. My brother, Mario, came up and was my best man. Dr. and Mrs. Kirby were very generous and made it an extra-special day for Beth and me. Peggy and Russell Goins also came up from Nebraska to stand in with me as my family. It was a very special day for me and proved to be the best decision I ever made in my life and probably the biggest risk Beth ever took. If she had only known what she was getting into...

After our wedding on October 3, 1981, we left Rochester, Minnesota, in my white 1980 Mazda RX-7 sports car on our way to a new life together. We were young and it was exciting. We were on our way to Shreveport, Louisiana, where I had a new job lined up. It worked out well because Beth's uncle was a doctor in Shreveport, and she had four cousins, all in medical school at the time, who lived there too. So off we went on our honeymoon, which consisted of our trip back from Rochester to Shreveport, Louisiana. We spent the first night in Hot Springs, Arkansas, at a little hotel by a river. We split an inexpensive dinner and a couple glasses of wine. But we were married and happy.

# Chapter 22
# The American Dream

Four months before our October wedding, I had been re-cruited to take over a fledging rental company in Shreveport by a young entrepreneur whose father had given him the business and just told him to do something with it. The son and I had met at a Curtis Mathes convention in Texas about six months earlier, and he promised to pay me well, and together we would build a national company with stores across America. I bought his line and moved to Shreveport the summer before Beth and I were married.

It didn't take me long to figure out that this father and son were not honorable people. They had no intention of building a national company with me. They only had one intention from the beginning for me: to use me to turn their failing business around so they could sell it for a good profit as soon as possible. Within four months, after I figured out their game, I found several inves-tors and Beth and I moved to Baton Rouge, Louisiana, so that I could open my own rental business. It was my first company. I thought, "This is it. I will rise above the ashes finally."

It had been my dream for a long time to own my own com-pany. I felt the American Dream was built on ownership, and I would never achieve any wealth unless I worked for myself. So, my newly found partners and I opened Gallery Rentals in the spring of 1982 in Baton Rouge, Louisiana. It was incredibly exciting for me. I knew I could not fail and I definitely was on my way.

On the night of the grand opening of our first store in Baton Rouge, Beth gave me some more good news: she was pregnant with our first child. She had gotten pregnant just three months after we were married and was about five months along. I was ecstatic. She was in shock, though.

The first store in Baton Rouge was a huge success. In less than six months we were planning the opening of our second store in Jackson, Mississippi, about three hours east of Baton Rouge. In September of 1982, we opened our second store in

Jackson, and it took off quickly too.

That first year was euphoric, especially when our daughter, Jane, was born. There is no way to put into words the incredible joy and change that our first daughter, Jane, brought into my life. "It changed both of us forever," we often said.

We had moved into a beautiful old home that we had renovated from top to bottom just before Jane was born in November of 1982. It was a storybook life unfolding in front of my eyes. I was there in the delivery room when she was born and I had never thought anything or anyone else was ever more beautiful in my life. It changed me instantly. "I will love you and make sure you have a good life," I said, as I held my baby girl in my arms that first time. She was an angel from God.

Along with the quick success I was experiencing came the challenges. My partners and I were starting to bicker about money and control. I had managed to buy up more than 60 percent of the company and that made them uncomfortable. I was never supposed to have more than 30 percent. However, when two of the original partners were bought out by the company, my share of the company grew substantially. I was now the president, controlling stockholder, and chairman of the board of Gallery, Inc. That was an uncomfortable situation for the other partners.

# Chapter 23
## "Come on America!"

In February of 1983, I made probably one of the craziest decisions of my life. It was a decision that would change Beth's and my life forever. It happened on my way back from our Jackson, Mississippi, store one warm southern Saturday afternoon in early February.

I can remember driving my custom van down the highway and enjoying the magnolia trees that lined the highway. They always looked green and pretty and I liked that drive. The sun shone down on the southern spring flowers that were already in bloom along the highway. Life was good.

I remember at first that I was anxious to get home and see the baby, since I had spent the night in Jackson. Like I did at that time, I had a cooler full of beer on ice in the van with me, and I had a marijuana joint in the ashtray ready to light. Soon, I had popped my second top on a beer, lit the joint, took a deep drag, and dropped off into my cruising mode, as I called it. I did this more and more at this time. When I really got buzzed, I thought my mind worked better and I was more creative, likable, and secure.

It was in that frame of mind that I came up with one of my craziest schemes in my life. On the radio there was a news clip about Ronald Reagan addressing a group of reporters out east. Apparently, Reagan got angry and told off one of the reporters who was out of line. Reagan had told the guy to shut up and sit down until he was called on to speak. It apparently raised quite a stir.

I was so enthralled by Reagan's guts, I got excited as I listened to the rest of the report. I had voted for Reagan three years earlier and liked his style a lot. I truly believed America needed him and we were lucky we got him in when we did. I remembered the state of the economy and the condition of our military prior to his election. I felt he was the right man for the time.

I was so enthusiastic about his reaction that I made the crazy decision right there in the car that I was going to write and produce a song in support of Reagan and get it on the air. I even jotted down a few of the lyrics on a piece of paper while I was still driving the van. I had never written or produced a song in my life. But I felt at that time that I could do anything I wanted and couldn't possibly fail.

The first person I looked up in Baton Rouge that day, before I even went home to see my wife, was my friend Perry Sanders, one of the first people I'd ever met in Baton Rouge. Perry owned a production studio, had spent time in Nashville, and had helped me produce the original jingle for the television commercials for my stores. (Produced on an 8-track on Perry's front porch, the jingle was a big hit locally.) Perry was the right choice. He loved Reagan, too, and his father was a friend of the Reagans.

In two hours Perry and I wrote the lyrics to the song "Come on America!" or "The Ronald Reagan Fight Song," as we also called it. When I got home that evening and told Beth what I was doing, she told me I was nuts. However, when she came to the final taping session with our baby and some of our close friends two weeks later, she was very surprised by how well it turned out. The song was impressive. Three weeks and $50,000 later, the song was pressed and we had 5,000 records in my garage. "What do I do with a Ronald Reagan song?" I thought, as reality set in on the magnitude of my crazy scheme.

As it turned out, one of the friends who was in the studio for the final taping session was so impressed, he told me one of his father's good friends was a fine southern gentleman by the name of (retired) General Robert H. Barrow. He would get the old general to help get it to Reagan in the following weeks on one of his trips to Washington. General Barrow had just finished serving as the Commandant of the U.S. Marine Corps (the highest ranking officer in the Navy and Marine Corps) and he had served on Reagan's Cabinet on the Joint Chiefs of Staff.

When General Barrow heard of my support of Reagan and heard the song, he was so impressed that he personally took the song to Washington and played it for Ronald and Nancy Reagan.

"The president and first lady liked the song very much,"

General Barrow told me. Later, I received a request to have the song scored for the Marine Band (the President's Personal Band). I also received a letter of gratitude from the Reagans. Finally, the song was later used during Reagan's reelection campaign in 1984. I never, however, made a dime off the 5,000 pressed records, which I later threw away. I did get some good local press in Baton Rouge at the time, which made me look good to my partners and my banker. It was a fun but expensive ride.

However, in the spring of 1983, the differences between my partners and I became even more apparent when at a board meeting I announced plans to open a third store in Mobile, Alabama, about four hours east of Baton Rouge along the Gulf Coast. The partners voiced their opinions about the concern of growing too quickly. They were worried about the large debt I was building to handle our inventory concerns and they wanted to see if the first two stores could sustain at least for another year and be profitable. "We are making money. So why push it?" they asked during the meeting.

The change that started in me in my early 20s was still there and it resurfaced its ugly head in a bigger way at about this time. I found myself motivated by money in a way I cannot explain. I also liked the feeling of power that control over the business and several million dollars a year gave me. I also found myself drinking more and smoking more marijuana again by myself in the car between stores. I could do no wrong in my mind and I was not going to listen to anyone. "I am the business," I thought to myself. "Their money is only as good as I'm working it."

"Ronald Reagan even likes me," I thought.

With complete board approval, after a major fight during the next board meeting, I forced my partners into the decision to open the third store and develop a franchise company in 1983.

I could tell my partners didn't care for me after that. "I don't care," I thought. However, I felt we could build this concept across the country in no time and franchising was the way to go because we could use other people's money. "I'll make them a bunch of money. They'll like me again," I found myself thinking. They agreed to go forward with the opening of the Mobile,

Alabama, store and the franchise company only because they were tired of fighting me.

In order to open the third store and develop the franchise package, which included a great deal of legal work, I spent another half-million dollars of our reserve cash and credit line before the doors were open in Mobile. The Baton Rouge and Jackson stores were holding their own. It was the fall of 1983, and fall was usually the good season of the year in the rental business.

Mobile soon opened and was making money. It got off to a great start. The franchise circular was being completed and I could get started selling franchises. It seemed like we were on our way.

# Chapter 24
## The party is over

In the spring of 1984, an uncontrollable series of events began to unfold that changed almost everything for me overnight. By this time we had a large but serviceable line of credit for inventory purchases with GECC and a revolving line of credit with a local bank. My banker and I got along well and things seemed great until the price of oil dropped by about $20 a barrel almost overnight.

Louisiana's entire economy at that time was based on the petrochemical industry, and banks and businesses that were deeply tied in (which were most) were in trouble. My bank was one of those that began to sweat almost right away. But my banker assured me nothing would change between us.

But everything did begin to change for me in late 1984. My bank went almost bust and was bought out by a New York bank. Ironically, Ronald Reagan's deregulation of banking was the kiss of death for my business. A New York-owned bank didn't give a damn about a little business in Baton Rouge, Louisiana. All they cared about was the bottom line. They didn't know me from Adam.

My banker, around whom I had built my business, was soon forced out of the bank by the new management. Not long after that, my line of credit with GECC was closed. That meant I could not purchase inventory for my stores anymore. I was on a slow deathbed. Then, to make matters worse, my partners had their names taken off the lines of credit with GECC. They could finally get me back for my greed and the fights we had. Now they could squeeze me out of the business. They felt I was out of control and I was going to take them down with me.

To add insult to injury, my franchises weren't selling, even though I was putting too much time and energy into the franchise business and neglecting the day-to-day business of running my company stores. Finally, I hired as a district manager a thief who eventually ran off with a lot of my money and also ran off my good help.

In February of 1985, I filed Chapter 11 protection in Federal Bankruptcy Court in Baton Rouge to try and hold on to the business. On that same day, I also received word that my father had died out in California. "How ironic," I thought. "My business, which is supposed to free me once and for all from my father's curse, is dead, and so is he. They have died together. He took my hope with him again," I reasoned. To top it off, Beth was pregnant again with our second baby. "Oh, my God. I am bringing another child into this world to suffer like I did. I can't take this," I thought.

Life couldn't get any worse than it was at that time for us. I couldn't look myself in the mirror, let alone my wife. Beth had never suffered in her life like she did then. We were broke and we had bill collectors after us. The bank even had the sheriff tow my company cars out of our driveway one day while I was at the bank trying to work things out. Beth was very pregnant and was just on her way to get some food when they drove up. The sheriff blocked the driveway so Beth could not drive off. They made her get out of the car and they hooked up the tow truck and hauled our cars away. Poor Beth just fell apart. I hated to see her suffer that much. It was terrible on her.

We soon found who our real friends really were through this. There weren't many. Our second baby Kate was born in October of 1985. She was the only joy we really had that year. But we were also scared and beaten down. One day, right after Christmas of 1985, while the pain of failure was overwhelming me, I almost lost it.

I remember sitting in the back porch of our house, which was Kate's nursery, and feeling hopeless. I knew I alone was responsible for what my family was going through. I had self-destructed and dragged my family down, just like my father did to me. I began to sob as I realized what I had done.

I had a shotgun in the garage and I went out the back door of the house to get it. I loaded the gun and went into the house. Beth and the kids had gone to the store. I kept thinking about that gun. I seriously kept thinking I had a half-million dollar life insurance policy on me and I was worth more dead than alive.

I could solve my family's problem real easy. But I also remembered what it felt like to grow up alone without a father. I went back and forth in my mind with this struggle. I somehow finally found myself asking God to help me. I hadn't really thought much about God for a while. At that instant, the thought came over me to call Sister Paul, from the orphanage, to whom I had not spoken for more than 18 years.

For some reason, I picked up the phone and called directory assistance for Joliet, Illinois. I got the number to the Mother House for the Sisters of St. Francis. I called and they located her. I was actually surprised she was still alive. I was very nervous while they went to find her.

Finally, I heard on the other line, "Hello. This is Sister Paul. Who's calling?" she asked. Her voice sounded just like it used to. She was sure and steady. It was good to hear her voice. I didn't quite know what to say, though.

"Sister Paul," I said, "this is Sal Di Leo. Do you remember me?" I asked.

"Sal Di Leo. How would I forget you and how are you?" she asked in her kind and reassuring voice. I felt alive again.

Sister Paul and I talked for almost half an hour. She asked me about my brother Mario and my sisters Kitty and Maria. I told her Maria had become a nun, too, and was living in California, and Kitty was living in Alaska and apparently doing well.

When she asked about me, I told her I was fine and doing OK. I didn't tell her how bad things were for me at the time. I think she knew somehow, that things weren't as I pretended. She asked, "Are you still going to church?"

"No, Sister. I left the Church," I said. "Then get back. Find a priest, go to confession, and receive Communion. You know you can't go through life without God," she finished.

I knew she was right. Tears were running down my face as I said I would and hung up. I went to the garage and hung the gun back up on the wall. When Beth and the kids came home, I hugged them a little tighter.

# Chapter 25
## Starting over in Minnesota

The Chapter 11 bankruptcy didn't work in Baton Rouge, and in the spring of 1986, broke and defeated, with a $7,000 loan from my father-in-law (who was very disappointed his daughter had to go through this), we moved to Minnesota to start over. I was 32 years old and Beth was 35 when we came to Minnesota in 1986.

This was a very challenging time for Beth and me. Coming back is no easy task, especially when you have no money or connections. I was a nobody in Minneapolis who now had no work history as an employee. I was a broke entrepreneur and no one wanted to hire me. I was considered a high risk.

If Beth ever had a good reason or chance to leave me, it should have been then. Why Beth didn't leave me I could never understand. I just waited for her to come home one day to break the news to me. We had moved into a two-bedroom apartment. We missed our beautiful home. We had to drive old rusted out cars. We had nothing but each other and the kids. It was not a good time for Beth. She worked as an audiologist and she brought in most of the income. I felt horrible for her and the kids.

I could only get poor-paying jobs. I was also very depressed and had lost most of my self-confidence. The only saving grace was that the kids were little and they brought us so much joy. There is not enough money in the world to substitute for the little joys our children brought us, even though we had nothing. I know that is what Beth and I survived on—our strong conviction for our kids and the fact that there was still love between us. It was a bittersweet experience.

One day I found out that I could make money helping other businessmen see what they were doing wrong, especially in the rental business. I understood how to build a good rental business—and how to destroy it. I was valuable to someone else in that industry. So I started a small consulting business. "Those who can, do. Those who cannot, teach," I remembered from a philosophy class at Nebraska. So, I taught and did all right with it. However, the more I got involved with other people's businesses, the more I wanted to come back and own my own business again. But I also wanted to come back fast, and I found myself looking for a home run. I got a taste of success once before, and I wanted it back quickly.

# Chapter 26
## Saving Ronald Reagan

One day, while I was feeling down and out and in a depressed state of mind, an opportunity jumped out at me right from the front page of the Minneapolis Star Tribune newspaper. It was during the Iran-Contra arms hearings in Washington, and Reagan was on the hot seat.

Even though I never did feel vindicated for the all the time and money I put into the Reagan song back in 1983, I always felt good about what I had accomplished. I also felt he was the best president we had had in a long time. Finally, I felt bad for him with the trouble he was in. I understood, in my own way, having just lost a business, what it felt like to take all the heat and be left alone at the top to fight it out.

"Honey, do you think I should re-launch the Reagan song? Maybe I can help Reagan and sell my records finally. Maybe I can make some good money," I said to Beth one night. "No," she said. "Stick to what you're doing and we'll work our way out of this mess." But I didn't want to listen to her. I felt like she wanted to hold me back.

The next day, I decided to put together a national grass roots movement in support of Reagan, using the song "Come on America!" as a rallying call. I called the campaign "Come on America!" of course.

At that time, I was consulting with a rental company in the Minnesota area that had five locations. The owner was an older gentleman who had a son my age. As it turned out, the son had some political experience, since he had been a speechwriter for a former Republican governor of Minnesota.

When I mentioned the idea to Randy Gustafson and his dad Verner at their corporate office the next night, I was surprised and excited by their reaction. They liked the idea and the song when I played it for them. They both appreciated Reagan, too.

Randy and I, with Verner's support, agreed to give it a try. We would launch the campaign in Minnesota within days. Randy soon proved he knew how to write press releases, set up press conferences, and how to pull the media's chain. We launched the campaign and held a press conference at the State Capitol building in St. Paul one Friday in early December 1986. We were local and national news overnight.

The ball got rolling fast after that. Beth was shocked and furious when I told her Randy and I were going to Fort Worth, Texas, the following week to duplicate the press conference during a Republican rally. Mrs. Eddie Childs invited us down and set the whole thing up.

Texas turned out to be bigger than we thought. Being a hard-core Republican state and having Vice President George Bush from there made it easy pickings as far as getting support from Republicans and the press.

We received a lot of local Texas press and some more national press. We made national television and a lot of newspapers across the country, and we were even mentioned in Newsweek magazine.

By this time letters of support and threats began pouring in. Bags of mail were showing up at the post office. It became a pain to open them. We were on our way, I thought. The only small problem was: who is going to finance this thing so we could continue? "I've got to keep the momentum going and I'll make some money off that record yet," I thought. I also thought people would just send the money in a flood. Letters continued to pour in, but with only a dollar here and a dollar there.

Within two weeks, Beth was running out of patience with me. I hadn't worked over those two weeks and she had received several threatening phone calls because of the campaign that really scared her. "Honey," I promised, "when we are through with the campaign, I'll be on every talk show in America and people will probably want to buy the record. We'll be in good shape again," I added. She wasn't convinced, but I went on with the campaign anyway.

Randy dropped out after the second stop in Fort Worth. He didn't like where I was going with the thing. He soon figured out I was more interested in promoting my own name and had my own agenda. So I recruited another fellow by the name of Mark, and we went on to Chicago.

There, in the liberal Democrat capital of unions and left-wing zealots, we got eaten alive by the press. They drilled us and attacked the campaign in every way possible. No supporters showed up to the rally. Even though we still got more national press, it was discouraging enough that Mark wanted out. He quit that day when we flew back to Minneapolis. I was too stubborn to quit. I had too much invested at this point. So I went to the Republican Party in Minnesota for help.

After the first rally at the State Capitol in Minnesota, we held an informal rally at the University of Minnesota for the Young Republicans of Minnesota. About 20 college kids showed up. In the group was a distinguished-looking middle-aged woman who stood out. After the rally, she introduced herself as Mrs. Evie Teegan.

Evie Teegan told me she was very active in the Independent-Republican Party of Minnesota and was impressed with what I was doing. She also told me she was a personal friend of Vice President George Bush. Finally she said, "If you need anything, feel free to call on me."

When we got back from Chicago, I didn't have anyone left to help me with the campaign or any money. So I called Evie Teegan. "Evie," I said, "I need money to continue this campaign."

"I can provide an airline ticket, hotel accommodations, and get support for you for one trip. But no money!" she said. "If you accept, you will go to Washington and hold a rally. I will get you in contact with a strong group of Reagan supporters there," she promised.

I was out of options. I had no choice. Even though I didn't feel good about going to Washington to face the most brutal press corps of them all, I felt I had to go. Again, I felt like I was too far into this thing to quit now. "Washington might be the big ticket," I reasoned with myself. With that I accepted her offer and she directed me to Washington, D.C.: right into Reagan's back yard during the Iran-Contra hearings.

It was a lonely and strange trip to Washington. Evie set up appointments for me with active Republicans around Washington. The next day I had meeting after meeting and tried to get their support. I met also with Maureen Reagan, who was active in the Republican Party. They all looked at me like I was crazy, but gave me the "go get them" pat on the back. I felt like I was putting myself up to be a lamb going to the slaughter. But for some reason, I kept on going.

Then I went to the White House. It was a rush meeting with two of Reagan's staff members. I was disappointed with the treatment I received. It was like 'good job, boy. Keep up the good work.' "The President is too busy to see you right now and so is Vice President Bush," a White House spokesperson explained. In the meantime, Oliver North was being grilled on the Hill and it was on every television station in Washington.

Finally, that night I set up for the press conference at the Republican national headquarters. Not one of the people I met with that day showed up for the press conference, or any Republicans from anywhere. The press did, however, and they let me have it worse than Chicago.

"Aren't you feeling a little ridiculous that you don't have any supporters here with you for your so-called 'Come On America to save Ronald Reagan' campaign?" one reporter asked.

"No," I said. "They're all afraid of you guys. But I'm not because I really believe Ronald Reagan is the best president this country has had in a long time, and I am here to let you know that. I'm also here to tell you I have many letters from Americans across the country who feel the same way I do, and we're not going to let you destroy him."

By this time, however, inside I felt like I had failed Reagan, my wife, and me. Even though I was disappointed at the outcome and knew this was the end, I felt glad I got a shot back at that reporter and all the rest of them in the room that night, maybe for Reagan or maybe for me. I wasn't even sure at that point. The rest of the conference was a blur. Surprisingly, I managed to handle the barrage and made national news again with the campaign.

I left Washington that night disenchanted and feeling defeated. I got home late on December 23, 1986, and never went out on the campaign again. When I got back to Minneapolis, I promised Beth I would never do the Reagan deal again. Beth was still there for me. She never left. "She must love me more than I think," I thought as I lay in bed that night. "I wish she would leave me. It would be easier," I also thought.

After my battle for Ronald Reagan, I decided to stay away from politics forever. "It is thankless and there is no loyalty to anyone from anyone," I told Beth. Not too long after that, Reagan made it through the fire and Iran-Contra was over. We got nothing in return. I somehow felt I should have received some form of gratitude from him or the party. I also thought they must have felt it was best to distance themselves from a loser like me once I had done my job. I guess I felt like I had made a national fool out of myself. I also felt that maybe they thought I looked too zealous for Reagan to be associated with me, even if I might have helped him. Who knows? I really did think a lot of Reagan and did want to help him. I was just hoping I could get something out of it, too.

When I finally had time many months later to reflect on what had happened, I called Randy Gustafson again and asked him if he thought anything good ever came out of the campaign for Reagan. "We made a difference. You scared them just enough in Washington to back down," he said.

Somehow I knew Randy was right. Not long after my trip to Washington, the press seemed to buckle a little and Oliver North came out of it. So did Reagan. I guess I felt it wasn't worth trying to prove to anyone what we had done. "Who would listen and why would they care?" I asked myself after I hung up the phone. I just stared at the wall in silence. I was drawn to the picture of Beth and me on our wedding day and relived it over again in my mind for a few long moments.

# Chapter 27
## Get up again and fight

I found myself looking for another business soon after the Reagan episode. It has always been my insecure need to have a unique business, something that hasn't been done before. I was born an entrepreneur and I knew it. "Maybe I could finally make it if I really come up with something unique," I told a friend of mine one day.

It wasn't long before I found a partner and we opened an antique store: a "rent-to-own" antique furniture store. I thought people would jump on this one, too. Within three years, this business was finally starting to make money and it looked like I might make it well. Nothing earth-shattering, but as the concept caught on via word of mouth, it became pretty successful. Lots of attorneys came to us to furnish their offices, and our show-room and back-room space eventually grew to 12,000 square feet.

One day, not long after things started going well, a shock hit me between the eyes again. My 49-year-old partner dropped dead of an aneurysm. To make matters worse, I ended up getting beat out of the key man insurance policy we had on each other by her ex-husband and her sons. She was the investor and had the credit and capital to make the business work. Without her, I was in no position to make a go of it financially. On top of it all, she had been a dear friend to my wife and children. She was like part of our family.

My partner's ex-husband convinced his sons to sue us for all of the assets of the business, including the $150,000 policy we needed to make the business continue. Beth and I were so upset by the loss of our partner and by the brutal behavior of her sons, of whom we had thought a great deal, that we didn't have the fight in us to try and protect ourselves. We thought it was best to walk away. So we did. We were broke again. It was 1991 and I was 35 years old. Beth was 38 and she still stayed with me. The kids were still little, but this time, they were big enough to understand we were broke. It was tough.

I am not sure if I am incredibly brave or just bull-headed. But it was at this time, by an unusual stroke of luck, that I met Bud Grant, the former Minnesota Vikings football coach. Bud turned out to be one of the most influential persons in my life in a way no one else had ever been, other than maybe the nuns back at the orphanage. He was kind, straightforward, had a great way of giving sound advice, and he wasn't stuck on himself. I was awed by him every time I met with him. I couldn't believe he had the time for me. It gave me the lift I needed to believe in myself again and the push I needed to get up again and try.

I had decided I needed a spokesperson for a new product line that I was trying to develop for the outdoor market, not too long after the antique store was lost. I had seen Bud Grant in some outdoor magazines as a spokesperson; one day, I cold-called him. I was surprised that he took my call, and we met for lunch over in St. Paul. I was awestruck the first time I met him. To be with Bud Grant in public for lunch was exciting for me. People were staring at him. However, I soon learned that Bud was very cordial and proved to have a very keen sense of business. Somehow, he liked my idea and that day we managed to work out the beginning terms of an arrangement with him as the spokesperson for the outdoor product line.

He didn't try and step on me like other people had done in the past. As a matter of fact, when I explained to him about how many times I had failed or been beaten down, Bud encouraged me to go out and try again. Probably not unlike the advice he would have given any one of his players during a game when they were down. I could see why the guys who played for him gave so much. You hated to let him down because he trusted in you so much.

That business relationship led to the beginning of several other business dealings with Bud and the beginning of a great friendship. Bud has proved to be a consistently great guy who has helped me gain the confidence and sense of well-being that I needed to believe I could succeed. I felt that I could go the distance now with Bud behind me.

In 1994, I sat on my front porch of our small but happy

home in Minneapolis on a warm July day and listened on the radio to Bud Grant's acceptance speech into the NFL Hall of Fame. It was a great speech. Bud got choked up. What struck me the most was how Bud gave all the credit to his family and the players and friends around him. "The Kid Finally Made It" was a very touching speech. I cried because I was so proud to be Bud's friend and appreciated his trust in me when everyone else turned their backs on me.

Three-and-a-half years later, on a dark and windy December day in 1997, I was working my car toward the Minnesota Vikings headquarters. The light Minnesota snow was falling softly on my windshield and was melting on contact as I drove in the night. I could hear the heater blowing hot air on the windshield and the back-and-forth sound of my windshield wipers as I moved along almost in trance. I was nervous about what was on my mind and what I was about to tell Bud. I remember the wipers sounded like they were singing a broken tune as they bumped to the left and then bumped to the right. They had a beat and sound of their own. The glare from the lights of the cars in front of me on the melting snow on my windshield and the back and forth motion of the wipers put me into another world all my own as I drove along in the darkness. It was almost as if the car was driving by itself as I thought about what I was going to tell Bud that night.

Several months earlier, Bud and I had started another project together that looked like it was going to be fun and promising. We were putting together the State Fish Art Contest for kids. We designed it to mirror the Federal Junior Duck Stamp Program that was so successful across the country. Our program was designed to teach kids across America conservation education using art as a springboard. "This project feels good and it's going to be fun, Bud," I said. "I am going on to the IEG Conference in Chicago with Mike Tvrdik with Mall of America and I will be meeting with AOL there in March." I added. "I will put together some great sponsors on this thing, Bud, and I just like the way this one feels because it isn't about money this time. I like what it does." Bud agreed.

111

While I was in Chicago at the conference, I thought I might stop in and see somebody very important from my past—a profound figure to say the least. First, however, I wanted to get some advice from Bud about meeting this person again, since it could open up the door to the single most important issue in my life, an issue I had to deal with to really be able to finally "go to the next level" with my life.

When I finally arrived at the Vikings office, all of the lights were out except a few in the lobby. Bud was waiting for me and he let me in. We went back to his office with all the sports trophies and pictures of him when he was a young professional athlete, as well as his eclectic collection of hunting and fishing memorabilia that lined the office. I always liked going in there because I would discover something new about Bud by just looking closer at an old picture or trophy. "Hey, Bud," I finally opened with in a rather shy manner, "remember when I told you I went to that Orphanage just outside of Chicago in Joliet when I was a kid?" I asked, as I finally sat across from him in his desk that night. "Well," I continued rather sheepishly, "I called down there today and found out it's not an Orphanage anymore. But when I called the convent where the nuns live, I found out that the old head nun from the Orphanage is still alive. Her name is Sister Paul," I added. "Do you think I should go back and see her? There are so many things I am still wrestling with in my mind about those days in the Orphanage and about my father deserting us," I finished.

Bud Grant has a way of looking through you when he is talking to you. He studied me for a moment and then said, "I think you should go back and face your bad memories and look for the good in your life. You were probably lucky you had that place to go to."

"I guess I will, Bud. I'll be nervous though. I haven't seen that nun or that orphanage for over 30 years. I have tried to put it out of my mind. I guess I'll call the old nun and see if she doesn't mind if I pop in," I finished uncomfortably.

112

# Chapter 28
## Back to the present

I found myself sitting out in front of the orphanage in the rental car again. I had been there for hours, losing track of time as I reflected back over the 35 years. I was stiff and a bit cold as I started the engine up to finally leave. The sun was just setting behind the Orphanage. It was as if the sun was telling me it was time to for us both to rest now.

As I drove slowly down the orphanage driveway, the old trees didn't look quite as old or as forbidding as when I drove in earlier that day. They just looked asleep.

I was exhausted and wanted to get back to the Chicago Hilton and to the banquet with Mike, Tasha, Sara, and the others from the Mall of America.

After reliving my life over in my mind that day, however, I had realized something very important. All along I had felt that I had a tough life and a lot of bad breaks. But somehow coming back here this day and really looking at it all over again I realized that I may have overlooked something very important.

"I have made it after all. I have Beth and the kids and a lot good friends. I also finally realize that all along the way, even during the darkest times, there always was somebody there for me like Sister Paul, Mr. Keenan, Dr. Magruder, Peggy and Russell, Bud Grant, Mike Tvrdik, and the list goes on," I thought. "I have been lucky," I thought with gratitude and a bit of relief.

When I got to the end of the driveway, instead of heading back towards Chicago, I turned the other way toward the retirement home for the nuns. It wasn't far from the orphanage, and I still remembered how to get there. I took one last look at the Orphanage in the rear view mirror.

I soon found myself parked out in front of Our Lady of Angels retirement home for nuns, where Sister Paul was staying.

I walked inside slowly, while the sun continued to drop off in the west. The March wind was blowing stronger now. The sunset caught my eye and the wind didn't chill me like it did earlier. It was a fading orange sunset of early spring. You could see it wanted to stay longer.

When I entered the building, I immediately noticed how it was decorated with pictures of Jesus and Mary. "Yep, this is a nuns' place," I said out loud to myself. I worked my way up to glassed-in front reception area with a woman in her 60s behind it.

"Excuse me. Are you a nun?" I asked.

"Why, no!" she said. "I am a volunteer. Is there something I can do for you?" she asked.

"Yes. I would like to see Sister Paul, if I could."

"Well, you probably can. She probably just finished dinner. It's 5:20 p.m.," she said as she looked up at the large clock on the wall behind her. "Does Sister Paul know you are coming to see her?" she asked.

" Yeah," I nervously answered. "I called her a few weeks ago and said I would try and come by today. I am a little later than I thought I would be," I added.

The woman looked at me and could see I was well-dressed and in a suit. I guess she figured I was all right. She picked up a microphone on the desk in front of her and said "Sister Mary Paul, please call the front desk."

It seemed like a long time, but was only about three minutes by the clock when the phone at the front desk finally buzzed. The woman picked up the phone and answered. "Hello. Yes, Sister Paul. There is a young man here to see you," she said into the phone and then looked up at me while she rested the phone on her shoulder. "What is your name?" she asked. "Sal Di Leo," I said rather shyly. "Sal Di Leo," she repeated into the phone.

At this point I almost wanted to turn around and get out of there. But something held my legs to the ground. At last I went over by the elevator doors behind me and waited about 10 feet from the doors.

As the elevator doors finally began to open, I began to get more nervous. Slowly, but steadily, out walked an old nun with a cane. Once she cleared the elevator she looked up at me. I was directly in front of her. " Hi, Sister," I said with a smile. "Let me look at you," she replied as she carefully studied my face. Then

114

she smiled.

"Tell me about your life, Sal," she said as she turned me around and we headed slowly up the long hallway past more pictures of Jesus, Mary, and angels.

"How much time do you have, Sister?" I asked.

"I've got eternity," she said, as we worked our way slowly down the hall.

"Sister, did I ever thank you?" I asked as we continued on down away from the bright lights of the front desk area.

"I'm sure you did, Sal."

# Chapter 29
## One more ghost to face

Seeing Sister Paul in Joliet was a wonderful awakening in my soul and a reminder of just how short life really is and how all things are connected, like it or not. The trip to see the nuns finally made me realize just how lucky I had really been to have been put into that Orphanage 35 years earlier. "You were one of the lucky ones," Bud Grant reminded me, when I got back and told him of what had happened.

Going back to see the orphanage again and old Sister Paul affected me in more ways than I could explain to anyone. Somehow, it was the beginning of a healing experience for me to finally begin putting things to rest that I had been struggling with all of my life. "It is a starting point for you," Sister Paul told me that night when I visited with her after all the years. However, Sister Paul reminded me on our long walk that night that I had to face one more thing. I had to try and find out what happened to my parents and I had to forgive them for the things that had happened that led to my being put in the orphanage. "Maybe you may never know the truth, but even if you don't, you need to finally give them redemption in order to finally move on," were the words she left me with.

I found myself being haunted by what Sister Paul had said after I got back to Minneapolis. Even though the trip had been the journey of a lifetime and I had finally come to grips with some very important issues, I still found myself feeling hollow and alone. The feeling of finally being at peace, which I had hoped to achieve by finally going back and facing my past, was still missing in my heart and my soul. "But why?" I found myself thinking when I got back home. "It should be over and I should be moving on," I found myself thinking over and over again. But it wasn't over, and instead of being free, I was more torn than I had ever been in my life. The experience in Joliet had reopened a chapter in my life that I had buried for years and forgotten. Instead of moving on, this forgotten chapter came alive again and only reminded me of the reality that I wanted to know more about what had happened to my family. Why had my father run off in the middle of the night back in 1963? He had always told us he was from the House of the Lion of Sicily and I carried the hope that it was true all through my years at the orphanage and at Boys Town in Nebraska. Now, instead of resting, I wanted to know the rest of the story again. I was torn between wanting peace at any cost or accepting the responsibility of finally finding the truth.

Three weeks later, March 1998...

The cab driver was a Middle Eastern man with a broken accent who kept looking at me in the rear view mirror as he drove along through the hustle and bustle of the mid-afternoon traffic. I was in awe of everything that was happening around me and was just trying to take it all in as I stared out the window.

I was looking for landmarks and trying to figure out where I was.

"You need to find No. 2 Charles Street in Greenwich Village," I reminded him again as I looked toward the meter on the front dash with concern. He noticed me looking at the meter, as he watched me in the rear view and started to be annoyed by my watching him closely. "I know where it is at," he said with irritation in his voice, while he stared back at me in the mirror.

I was worried because I had heard New York cab drivers took advantage of people by taking the long way to a destination, just to get the fare up. I only had a hundred dollars cash in my pocket and I had to make it last. The fare was already at $27, I had no idea where I was, and I was a bit nervous.

After a while, I found myself thinking about the last time I had seen my mother alive, back in 1989. That was 9 years earlier and I was trying to remember clearly what had happened when most of my brothers and sisters had gone to see her, to pay our last respects. It was a quickly arranged family reunion at my older brother Mike's place in Union City, Pennsylvania.

My brother Mike had called us all to tell us that our mother was dying of cancer and we should all come to Pennsylvania for a Di Leo Christmas reunion to say goodbye to our mother and put some things to rest. Mike and his wife Valerie had taken her in and had finally given her a home of her own toward the later part of her life. She had finally had some happy years the last 10 years of her life and had finally felt good about herself as a grandmother to their children. They had given her another chance and I have always appreciated what they did for our mother and our family. Mike and Valerie were amazingly strong people and they were kind to have done what they did for our mother.

Before that reunion in 1989, I hadn't seen my mother for more than 20 years and had seen very little of her before that after being put into the orphanage back in 1963. Surprisingly, 10 of her 12 children showed up for the reunion, ranging in age from 31 to 51. Most of us had seen very little of our mother and very little of each other before we arrived for the reunion. It was the first time that most of us had been together in over 30 years and we were all wanting to find out about each other and catch up on each other's lives.

It was a bittersweet reunion as I think back on it. It brought out in all of us, I am sure, mixed emotions. I am quite sure we were all secretly wondering how we all felt about each other and were also wondering what we were all dealing with in our lives at the time, as well as what we had been through to get to this point. It was a chapter in time that will never be reproduced or even truly comprehended.

Time stood still for those few days. I was so happy to be with these people whom I was pulled away from at such a young age and whom I had wished over and over again to be with every day I was in the orphanage and at Boys Town. Now, I was finally with them, and as I looked around the room the first night, I saw middle-aged adults, not the young brothers and sisters I had missed for all those years. It was nice and it was also strange.

In our family, I was the second youngest of the 12 kids and I was 34 years old at the time of the reunion. Our sister Angie was the oldest at the reunion and was in her early 50s. Our brother Chuck, the oldest, had elected not to come to the reunion and we were all disappointed about that. However, Angie looked very weathered and old I thought when I saw her. She had had a rough life over the years and it was apparent in the way she looked and the way she acted. I was sad for her because I remembered when I was at the Orphanage how she would come and get Kitty and me and how young and vibrant she was. I never forgot that and always appreciated it. She was healthy back then. Now, she was overweight, smoking a lot, and looking beaten down and unhappy. She just sat there most of the time on the couch, looking off into some other place in the wall or on the ceiling. My heart was heavy with her sadness but I didn't know what to do to help her.

During the course of that seven-day reunion, however, we managed to laugh a lot, too. I especially loved hearing for the first time some of the incredible stories of our family before I was born. Jerry, Tony, Angie, Ross, and the other older ones told us stories about our father and the crazy and unfathomable episodes of how we lived when they were young. We could only laugh and shake our heads in disbelief at what they had gone through in the 40s and 50s, before the "old man" (as they called him) split for good in '63. I found myself so amazed with the stories that I tried to not miss any of the discussions on the family as they came up.

Some of the stories that came up during these conversations were hard ones to listen to. They were the ones I had not heard and that brought back the old terrible feelings of despair and powerlessness that I had felt as a child and had long put out of my mind. As I listened, I found my stomach starting to tense up, and I wanted to walk away. But my curiosity kept me there and I knew I had to face these mixed-up feelings of fear, anger, despair and sadness in order to go on with my life. I kept listening to my brother Jerry, more than anyone, since he was the second oldest at the reunion (almost 14 years older than me). He was more inclined to tell about the more difficult times and situations our family went through before I was born. He and Angie, the two oldest at the reunion, knew the most.

As we sat listening to Jerry and Angie in my brother Mike's living room one afternoon when my mom wasn't there, one story stuck me right in the heart and I felt a sense of sadness that I am not able to describe here in words. I think this story told it all about my mother's despair and how we kids were trapped with her in her helplessness.

The room was filled with smoke, since most of my siblings were heavy smokers. As I tried to breathe and listen the smoke hung in the air and created an atmosphere of stale air and a sense of timelessness. The smoke didn't seem to move but set up a pattern of grayness. My sister Angie was looking at the floor as she sat on the couch with a cigarette in her hand. She said almost to herself, "I am so glad Mom finally got to see all of us together and that we are all OK." With that, we all stared down at the floor and the room got almost perfectly still. We found ourselves looking over to Jerry for more. Jerry knew we younger ones were hungry for more information and he took a deep drag off his cigarette and let the smoke out of his lungs slowly to add more corruption to the already dead air in the room. He seemed to be looking off nowhere before he started talking. For a long few seconds the room was completely silent as his gaze drew us all into the mood.

"Mom was so abused," he said slowly and seriously as he looked off and sighed. Then he stared right at me and with a low and subtle voice he continued on as we were all drawn into the window of his mind. "She had such strong faith, though, and I don't know why. When the conditions she was in were too much for anyone to bear, she somehow managed to hang on. I guess somehow God must have heard her desperate little voice," he continued. With that, I could see my sister Maria, the nun, put her face in her hands and start to tremble as she silently wept. Jerry saw this and paused for a second, but from our looks, he knew he had to go on.

"Sally," (as he affectionately called me), "you weren't even born yet, but to give you some idea of how bad it was, one day, back in the late 1940s, we were in a rusted-out old car traveling through Alabama. I don't even know what we were doing there to begin with. Anyway, we were on our way to Florida, I think to look for a place to live and start over again. We had run out of gas on the old two-lane highway and Dad had gone off to beg someone for gas when a state trooper saw the car and stopped to check it out. As he approached the car he must have seen all six of us kids in the car with Mom. We were all hungry that day because we hadn't eaten for at least a day-and-a-half, and my stomach hurt. I can remember the trooper sticking his head in the car to check us out, and he could see it was a bad situation. He asked Mom what was going on and she told him we were out of gas and food and that Dad was off to try and get some help. The trooper asked Mom where we were going and Mom told him. 'Ma'am, how can you travel with all these kids with no money and food?' he asked in a pitying sort of way.

"'God will provide for us,' was all Mom could say in her helpless little voice. I can remember the surprised and sad look on the man's big face as he stared in disbelief at us all. He slowly reached for his wallet and gave Mom some money and headed off to get some gas for us. When he returned with a can of gas, Dad had already come back empty-handed. After the tank was filled, we drove off staring out the back window at the trooper while he looked back at us kids in the back seat. I can remember being so happy to eat a bologna sandwich that evening that Mom had bought at a Piggly Wiggly. I don't know how Mom could have handled the terrible stress and conditions we were in. She must have been so overwhelmed and yet somehow hung on to her faith. To this day as I think back on those terrible years I think she was either completely out of her mind from all the despair and couldn't even think or she truly somehow hung on to the hope that God would really somehow answer her little prayers." With that he took another deep drag, stared off into nowhere again and slowly let out more smoke from deep down in the bottom of his being. We all sat there in silence as we relived our mother's pain with him.

"Dad never worked a decent day in his life. Mom carried the hope he would all through her life. I am glad he ran away for good in '63," Angie said in anger. "You little ones were better off in that orphanage."

After a few moments of silence, we all tried to get beyond the painful memories and started to try and lighten things up. With that I recalled one thing about my childhood before I went into the orphanage.

"Mike," I said in a lively voice to help lighten the load, "do you remember how you would make yourself the self-appointed godfather of us boys when we moved into a new neighborhood? As soon as we got unloaded you would get us together and assign us to groups of two with a strategy of combing about a one-mile radius of our house. We would be sent out to scout out the new neighborhoods to map out every vegetable garden, apple tree, cherry tree or fruit bush around, with a general idea of when they could be carefully harvested. We never left home in the summer without a salt shaker in our back pocket, and while other kids in the neighborhood lost their winter fat, we gained weight like squirrels for the upcoming winter."

With that, the whole room was smiling and laughing. I loved them all in that room because we had gone through it together. "We were like Tom Sawyer and Huck Finn a hundred years later," Mike said as every one of us laughed hysterically. "We were a baseball team and gang all in one," Mario added, and Vince threw in, "No one messed with us Di Leo boys."

After a few days at the reunion, I decided I needed to start writing things down so I could get events straight and not forget anything. I wanted to know so much because I knew so little. On the fourth day of the reunion, I heard something in a conversation that began to awaken my soul and haunt me all over again like it had when I was a child at the Orphanage. I heard my brother Mike say that our mother and father had come from good families. That statement ripped right through my heart because I had put it out of my head for so many years as being nonsense and now after hearing Mike say it, it renewed my burning desire to know if it was true and what had gone wrong. I wanted to know the truth.

On the day after Christmas, when everyone had gone for a walk in the fresh Pennsylvania snow, I got my chance to learn more about what had happened to our family.

The reunion was a nostalgic time for all of us, and we all found time to go off with one another and spend some personal time to get to know more about what had happened in each other's lives over the years. As a matter of fact, we found ourselves doing this a lot and tried to get to each other one-on-one as much as possible before time ran out. Deep down, I am sure we were all grateful to have had this incredible moment in time together, a moment we never thought we would see in our lifetimes. As a result, we used every minute of our time with precious gratitude. It was as if we had been prisoners of war and we had finally been reunited with our family.

On December 26, I found myself alone in the house in the early afternoon. A fair amount of new snow had fallen the night before and in the early morning, and my brothers and sisters had decided to go for a walk in the new-fallen snow. I found myself with no one left in the house but my mother, who was in bed. So it wasn't long before I found myself thinking about our family and what had happened. I wanted to know so much. It wasn't long before I was going down the hall with my pen and notepad in my hand to see my mother.

When I got to her door I knocked and heard a soft, "Come in." As I opened the door, I could see a faint little body on the bed, with her head up on a couple of pillows, looking out the window into the softly falling snow. "Mom, is it all right for me to come in?" I asked. I could tell right away that she was not feeling well and was a bit under the weather. "Oh sure, Sal," she said. "Please come in and sit with me," she added with a little sigh of happiness in her voice.

As I slowly went into the room I could see her study my face while I moved closer to the bed. I sat down on the edge of her bed and picked up her little hand and held it in mine. We both just smiled awhile and said nothing for what seemed like a long time. It must have only been a minute, however. She then turned and looked out the window again and watched the snow softly falling. You could see a couple of kids off in the distance sledding down a hill. Mom then said, "I always love this time of the year. I have always hoped to see all my children again, home for Christmas. God has given me that before I die. I am very grateful," she finished as she continued to look out the window. With that, tears started rushing down my face as I quietly held on to her hand and looked out the window with her.

"Mom," I said, "I love you and want you to know that I hold no hard feelings about what happened to me. I am probably luckier than the others to have gone into the Orphanage," I added slowly but steadily. "I am glad I am here with you and have had a chance to be with the rest of my family, too," I also said, as the tears continued to drop in my lap.

"Don't cry, Sal. I am at peace with what has happened and how it has all turned out."

"Mom," I finally said, "I just need more answers about our family and how things ended up like they did."

"Were we from a good family and what happened to Dad? When I was little, I remember him saying he was from the 'House of the Lion' from Sicily. I have carried the hope that was true all my life so I could hold my head up high. Was that true, and why did he run off?" I finished.

She started to tell me the story about our family, going back to the early 1900s, and I found myself mesmerized by it all. It was like another person's family history being told and could not have been my own. I wrote as fast as I could on the notepad and promised over and over again as I wrote that I would do a family history and get a copy to all of our family members some day.

Her story went like this. "When the Stock Market crashed in 1929 and the rich and famous lost their millions, it became a customary sight in New York City to witness their un-parachuted bodies flying down from the high-rises and hitting the sidewalks as the Depression got started, as was told to me by my future in-laws, Sarafino and Colegaro Di Leo," she said. "I think they had told me that so we could understand why they were broke at the time, too. They had apparently lost their life savings of $5,000 to the bank and so the mother wasted no time in hopping the first ship to Sicily and returned to the U.S. with their teenage son (your father), Anthony, whom she immediately set to work at a sewing machine in a garment factory where he learned the trade. Your father brought home weekly checks that he dared not cash himself, not even a nickel of it, for fear of his life. Your father was from a town in Sicily called Ribera, in the province

125

of Agrigento, and he was reared by his mother's parents until he was brought over to the States. Their names were Angela and Rosario Burno.

"My parents, Mose Perniciaro and Josephine Piscitelli, were also from Sicily. My father was born in Mazara and my mother hailed from Messina, Sicily. She unfortunately died at the age of 22 from the Spanish Flu epidemic of the First World War, in 1919, along with her son, my brother, Jerome, who was 2. My father then married Catherine Elari, from a family of 16 children, all born in Marsala, Sicily. His brother, my Uncle Salvatore, whom you are named after, also lost his first wife to the Spanish Flu and then married my stepmother's sister.

"My stepmother was good to me, and she cleaned both apartments where we lived, ours and uncle Sal and my cousin Santa's on the third floor. She also took care of us both during the day, including cooked for both families. We were raised like sisters. In the meantime, my aunt, her sister and Santa's stepmother, worked in the family pastry shop down on the main floor of the building with the two brothers, since she had had business experience back in the old country. We had a good family business and both families lived quite comfortably in our city apartment building which we owned, as well as we had a beautiful home on the ocean in which my cousin and I spent most of our summers growing up."

As she continued to tell her story, I couldn't help but notice how affectionately she referred to her father and stepmother. She had a special smile on her face, as she would allude to them. "She must have loved them very much," I thought.

Then, my mother continued, "I met your father at an event called 'Dancing Under the Stars,' held every Saturday night in Central Park. A good band was playing in the park gazebo and I was there with my cousin Santa and two more girls. It was there that I met Anthony Di Leo. He was very handsome, but was not dancing because he did not know how. As time went on, I continued to see him, to the terrible dislike of my father, and yet I still married him," she finished. By this time, she was very tired and wished to go to sleep.

"Mom, can you tell me why your father didn't like him and was he from the 'House of the Lion'?" I asked. But I could see she did not have the energy to go on so I tucked her in. I thanked her for the time as she drifted off to sleep and bent over to kiss her on her forehead. I was grateful to have the information I had, but I wanted to know so much more. I wanted to know what had happened to her after she and my father got married and what happened to her mother and father. I would try again later that week, I thought, but the opportunity never came up again.

When I got back to the living room, I could hear my brother Vince coming in the front door with my sister Maria, who was raised in the orphanage with me and who had become a nun. They were laughing together and had just come in from a walk together. It was so spiritual to see us all together again, trying to bring our lives together again as a family for that one precious week. We were all happy and sad at the same time. None of us wanted it to end.

I didn't even know my mother had a cousin until that week and I also found out she had written to her cousin Santa when she learned of her illness and that the two of them finally communicated after many years. Apparently, they had made amends and talked a great deal about a month or so before the reunion. Mom gave me Santa's address and phone number on the last day I was at the reunion. My brother, Mike, brought it out of the bedroom from her for me to have. My mother died of cancer three months later and that was the last time I saw her. Now, just one month after I came back from seeing the Nuns at the orphanage after 30 years, and eight years after my mother's death, I found myself going to Greenwich Village to see Santa Isola, my mother's cousin, the only person left alive who knew much about my mother's childhood and what had happened to my grandparents.

My mind drifted back to the cab ride as we headed to Santa's apartment in Greenwich Village. I found myself rehearsing over and over again what I would say to her when we finally met for the first time. I had written to her on several occasions and even called a couple of times to see if she would help me find some of the answers. Now, I was finally going to meet her in person. I was very nervous about what I would find and how she would receive me.

I found myself back in the cab thinking about the cab driver. "It should be over there," I said out loud. I startled him since I had been quiet for so long. I had noticed at $37 on the meter that he was trying to run the meter up. I had noticed that we had crossed Charles Street but he acted like he hadn't noticed. That had been a while ago. Finally, he pulled up in front of an old brownstone apartment building in Greenwich Village. I saw Number 2 in brass on the old door at the top of a small set of steps in front of the building. The whole block the building was on was like a page out of a history book. I had seen pictures of old New York neighborhoods from the turn of the century, and here I was as if I had gone back in time. On that block, with all those old buildings, it was as if time had stood still.

"I am not paying you more than $37," I said before the driver could say anything. "I saw you cross over Charles Street twice a while back and I don't think I should be charged for more than $37 because that was on the meter when you crossed it," I finished in a firm voice. I paid him just $37 and he was angry with me, needless to say.

After my run-in with the cab driver and reliving in my mind the last time I had seen my mother alive, as well as the anxiety of soon meeting Santa, I was very exhausted. "I hope I can get through this," I thought. I was very much on edge. I rang the doorbell and finally could see a thin man, probably in his 70s, with a little European hat on, coming down the stairs to the door. "That must be Santa's husband, Neal," I thought.

The man opened the door with a smile and said, "You must be Sal. I am Neil." He had a very pleasant voice and was casually dressed in a pair of nice but comfortable pants and a sweater. I immediately liked him. There was something calming about him and he took the edge off the incident with the cab driver and my fears of not being welcome. "Come in. Come in and get acquainted with your cousin," he said. "Thank you," I replied as I followed him up two flights of stairs in the old building.

As we neared the top of the stairs, I could see a door open, and a small woman, not more then 5 feet tall at the most, neatly dressed with her hair done up nicely, and in her 70s now. She looked rather pleasant and was just waiting for Neal and me. As we mounted the last steps and headed for the door, Neil said, "Here is your cousin, Santa. Say hello to Sal," he finished, almost out of breath from his climb.

I stood there for a moment and had to take a second look. She looked so much like my mother. "Hello, Sal," she said in a nice voice. Then she asked, "Did you have a nice trip?"

"Yes," I said. "It is so nice to finally meet you. You look so much like my mother," I added. With that she smiled at me and Neal said, "Come in and get acquainted. You have so much to talk about."

As I entered the old apartment in Greenwich Village, I could see pictures of people on a set of bookshelves and on the old buffet. "That must be her family," I thought. The apartment was rather warm-looking, but by no means fancy. They offered me a seat and something to drink. As I reached for the Coke Santa brought in I tried not to show I was nervous and that I was all right. I also wanted them to know that I felt good about who I was and that I didn't want anything from them but information. Neal immediately tried to get us to talk while he watched with a rather playful attitude.

"Santa," I finally said, "Can you tell me more about my mother and my grandparents? I am looking for answers from the past and you are the only one who can help me." At that Santa was a bit cautious and she asked, "What do you want to know?"

"I want to know what happened to my family, going back to the beginning," I said. "Would you mind telling me what you know?" She looked at Neal, who at this question sat up in his armchair and looked back at her with a smile, but a bit more serious. He then nodded slowly at Santa in approval and she began telling me what she remembered.

"Your mother and I were raised as sisters and we knew each other well. My father, Salvatore, whom you were named after, and your grandfather, Mose, ran our family business together and they worked hard and gave us a good life here," she went on. As she continued, I realized I was hearing the same story over again that my mother had told me almost nine years earlier, just before she died. However, the differences in their stories finally came out when it came to my father.

"Your mother should never have gone out with him, let alone marry him. He was a strange person and none of us, my friends and I, liked him. He was so old country and didn't seem like he was able to talk to you. However, your mother fell for him, despite her father's pleading not to get involved with him. I think your mother was so spoiled by her father after the death of his first wife and his son, that her father may have been over protective of her and he spoiled her. So maybe she rebelled. Maybe that is why she didn't listen to her father and married Antonio any way. It wasn't long after she married him that she was pregnant with her first child and it only got worse from there. He couldn't hold a job and so your grandfather lent him money to help him out. It even got worse yet. Your mother continued to get pregnant and your father continued to prove he didn't want the responsibility of taking care of a family and things went from bad to miserable. All the while your grandfather watched his daughter go deeper and deeper into the pits of poverty. Now you have to understand that Catholics didn't dare get divorces in those days and parents from good and hard working families would do anything to help their children keep their status in life. However, when you mother's life went down the tubes and they became poverty stricken with a bunch of kids, on a cold winter's day in 1942, your grandfather, Mose Perniciaro, at our summer home on Long Island, in East Patchogue, New York, took the life of his second wife Catherine Elari and then his own. His brother Salvatore, my father, was the first to discover the bodies when they were missing and he then called the authorities," she finished and looked at the floor as she told this part. "I think your grandfather was so depressed about what had happened to your mother, and the fact that he had some problems with depression, that he couldn't take it any more," she added.

Then she showed me some pictures of their summer home on Patchogue that her father and my grandfather had built. It was a beautiful estate with big flower gardens and wrought iron fences. She showed me pictures of her children, my long lost second cousins at the estate in the 1950s in the summer. I could see how well their lives were going and couldn't help thinking that in the 1950s we were dirt poor, and by the time I was born in 1954, we had 11 kids. Kitty was born in 1956 and we were beyond the poverty level. We were moving, as my brothers and sisters had said at mom's family reunion, as fast we could to stay just ahead of the law and away from landlords who had us evicted. By the 1950s, my mother's life was in shambles and we were there with her, helpless, powerless, and hopeless. I couldn't help but feel the pain again when I saw pictures of my cousins on the beautifully manicured lawn, as I remembered back to my childhood. I also felt the pain for my mother as well and almost wished I wasn't there to see all this.

"Santa," I finally said after a minute of silence in which we all just looked at the floor, "Do you think my father really came from a good family? Was he really from the House of the Lion as he told us when we were little?" I finally asked.

Santa took a breath and carefully chose her words, "I think your grandparents on your father's side were hard-working people. They were uneducated, but not bad people. Your father had a tendency of not telling the truth and your mother had a tendency of wanting to believe him. I think they were bad for each other. I don't think there ever was any 'House of the Lion,' as your father called it."

With that, I got up heavy-hearted and thanked both her and Neal. I was so grateful to them for spending the time with me and yet I was very heavy-hearted to have to hear all this. Neil, being the kind soul he was, offered to walk me down to Bleecker Street where the bakery was that my grandfather and his brother had built their business. "Come on now," he said as he tried to make me feel better and Santa comfortable, "That was years ago and now you're back together again as family!"

I appreciated Neal's kindness as we walked to the old apartment building on Bleecker Street where my grandfather and his brother had their bakery business downstairs and where my mother and her cousin Santa grew up.

It was cold out now and the sun was going down. I could tell Neal was not in the best of health and he was trying so hard to make me feel welcome. We walked to the old building and I just stared up at it, all three stories of a building where almost a century ago two families' lives had played out on the same stage. One family had a good ending and one family came apart. I just looked hard for several minutes and tried to understand what had happened. I wished I could go back in time and fix things. As we turned away to leave, my heart was heavy as we talked about little things on the rest of our walk. About then, the sun dropped off behind the old buildings in Greenwich Village like the lights going out on a dusty, old, inner-city stage set. I knew it was time to go, but I didn't feel I was ready for the ending I had found. Neal was a kind man and I could tell he was hoping I would feel good, and I appreciated it as we lumbered along the cold, dark street and I finally waved down a cab.

On the plane back to Minneapolis that night I couldn't sleep, even though the lights were out and everyone else was quiet. I replayed over and over in my mind what had happened that day and what I had learned. I tried to be relieved about finally knowing the rest of the story but there were too many emotions going through my mind at once. It was a heavy feeling. When we finally landed, I could only think of my lovely wife and wonderful children. "At least," I thought, "I have a life now and I know the truth. My father had run off for some reason that none of us but God will ever know," I thought. "Maybe he was scared, or maybe he was a bad person who was a coward. Anyway, it is too late to change all that now," I reasoned over and over all the way home to Minneapolis. It was like I was stuck with that thought but it didn't satisfy me. It only made me more angry and sad. Finally, as we landed in Minneapolis, I looked for my best friend to be there for me, just as she had been for so many years now. I looked for Beth to come and pick me up at the airport and there she was, waiting to give me a hug as usual and to see how I was doing. She was concerned about how I felt about what I had learned. "Beth is wonderful," I thought as we drove home.

# Chapter 30
## Pass it on!

I couldn't get out of my head, when I got back home, the incidents that happened in New York and what I had learned about my family history. Instead of giving me peace it only amplified my anger and my fears. It was troubling, to say the least, for several days. Beth was watching me closely and soon worried about me as she could see that I was struggling with it. Finally, after a few days, she suggested, "Maybe you should call Sister Paul and see what she has to say about it."

After a few more days of agonizing with it inside, I decided that maybe Beth was right. When I finally got Sister Paul on the phone, I told her what had happened. "I don't think it made any difference in my life to find out that my grandfather murdered my grandmother and then killed himself," I told her. "To top it off, I think my dad was a bum and my mother was a victim of a lot of bad circumstances, to say the least. Finding the truth didn't make any difference. It has only made me angrier," I said. "I think I got screwed and I am pissed off about it. Sorry to be so graphic with you, Sister," I added. "I am just not sure what to make of it all," I finished in a frustrated tone.

I talked to Sister Paul for about a half an hour in that tone and instead of getting upset or angry, she just let me talk it out. She only listened and acknowledged with a yes or a hum. After I had retold the whole story as best I could, she paused and then finally said very peacefully, "You have been blessed to get beyond what your mother suffered with and you are probably the answer to your mother's prayers in that you did survive and made it through. Forgive your father and mother for what happened and make sure your family doesn't experience that," she said. "If you can forgive your parents, you will have peace."

Somehow, I knew those words, as hard as they were to live by, were correct. They hurt me because I didn't want to forgive my parents or life in general for what it had dealt me. As we sat there in silence over the phone for what seemed like eternity, I remembered the words that Sister Nepomecine had said to me back many years ago at the orphanage when Mario had left for Boys Town. They seemed to jump out at me as if I was there again. "Sal, almost everyone in some way is dealt a bad hand in life. The people who do the best recognize that and, with the grace of God, make the best of what they have been given. You will do well with what you have. I just know it," she had said. As I remembered again those words of wisdom, of long ago, I wept over the phone with Sister Paul.

It was only she and I on the phone that night, and, I am sure, God also. I knew then that those old nuns were right all along and it was time for me to forgive and move on. My heart was heavy but filled with a newfound peace that I had never experienced. I was tired but relieved.

As Sister Paul and I finally wrapped up our conversation, she reminded me to make sure my children didn't experience the pain or anger I had dealt with. "You can bet they won't, Sister," I said enthusiastically.

Then she said one more thing. "Sal, remember to pass it on to anyone else who needs to know the truth!" she said. "I will, Sister," I replied. "I promise, I will," I assured her. "By the way, Sister," I added, "thank you."

January 1999, almost one year later....

As I sit here at my computer, upstairs in our small but happy home in Minneapolis, Minnesota, almost one year later, and as I finish writing this story down for someone to read someday, I can only say how happy I am today to be alive and have the life I now have.

It has been six days since I began writing this story down and hopefully my children and grandchildren will read it someday. I hope it will help them understand their past better and hopefully understand more about life in general. I also hope they will do better than I did and make smarter decisions about what success is and what is important in life.

Jane, my oldest daughter, who is a junior in high school, has agreed to help me with this book by editing it. She has been involved in a youth program with the Minneapolis Star Tribune newspaper and is an aspiring writer and journalist. She has already decided she will go to journalism school after High School. She is looking into the great journalism programs around the country and I am so happy for her.

I can hear our 14-year-old, Kate, downstairs playing the piano. She has been given the gift of music and she is quite the piano player and musician. She plays the violin and even writes her own poetry almost daily. She tells me musicians can't make a living so she is going to architecture school someday and will keep music as her hobby. I find it hard to believe these kids know so clearly where they want to go someday. I am sure they get it from their mother.

Beth is downstairs working on plans for our vacation to Mexico over the kids' spring break. It is truly wonderful to be alive and have the life I do now. I am very blessed.

As I have been writing all these things down from my life's journey, it has also made me wonder again about what has happened to some of the people who passed through. I would love to see Philip Belcher again some day and I hope he is doing well. After all, we were old foxhole buddies at the orphanage and at Boys Town. I wonder how Mary Fehrenbacker's life turned out, too. I'll bet she still has that sweet smile and probably has a couple of cute little girls of her own. I also wonder about some of my friends at the University of Nebraska whom I have lost contact with over the years and how they are doing. And the list goes on in my mind as I wind this thing down. It all seems so long ago and yet it has gone by so fast.

I am glad, however, that I have managed to keep in touch with some of the people along the way who were there for me, like the Raspolich family in Joliet, who took my sister Kitty and me home for the holidays when we were in the orphanage. I even exchange Christmas cards every year with Doctor Magruder and his family in Omaha. I know Ann is married now and has a family of her own. Her little sister Martha keeps me filled in with the Christmas card she sends me every year. Martha is still my little buddy and we have become pen pals over the past five years. Ann and I have never spoken since our college days in the University of Nebraska.

All of these people and all of these memories seem like ghosts from an incredible movie from someone else's life as I have reconstructed them for someone else to read about some day. Now, they are all connected.

When I am through with this book, I will send a copy to all of the wonderful people who were there for me along the way, like most of those I have just mentioned, the Goins family in Nebraska, and my good friend Bud Grant. I hope they are not embarrassed by it. I hope they will know how much I appreciate what they have all done for me. I am grateful.

**The End.**

# "Did I Ever Thank You, Sister?"

## Update, February 2000

Sal and Beth Di Leo are still happily married after almost 20 years and are living in Minneapolis, MN. Their two daughters Jane, 18, and Kate, 15, are doing exceptionally well in school with aspirations of professional careers in journalism and architecture respectively.

Mario Di Leo is happily married and is doing well in Dallas, Texas.

Maria Di Leo became a Catholic Nun and passed away after a courageous battle with cancer at the age of 39 in 1990. She will always be remembered.

Kitty Di Leo is well and living in Washington State. She has two wonderful children of her own.

Sister Mary Paul Korman O.S.F. suffered a severe stroke in the summer of 1998, but has battled back from the stroke and is doing amazingly well at the age of 87 years old.

Philip Belcher has never been heard from since Sal last saw him in the fall of 1973 when he came to visit Sal at the University of Nebraska in Lincoln.

Bud Grant has continued to be a good friend and mentor to Sal in business and life.

Sal and Jane Di Leo
Author and Editor
Father and Daughter
At the 2002 Rose Bowl

Beth and Sal Di Leo
Celebrating 20-years in 2001

Sal and his daughters Kate and Jane

141

Sal and Sister Rose. Who was the Sister in charge of the senior boys at the Guardian Home in the 1960's. This photo was taken in February 2001

Sister Paul at 87 with Sal.

Sal and Bud Grant
Sal presents Bud with a Customized
1994 NFL Hall of Fame Fly Rod

The old cottonwoods lining the driveway to the orphanage.

The old stone staircase to the Guardian Angel home orphanage.

The Guardian Angel Home

The Guardian Angel Home

The Guardian Angel Home

The Grotto at the Guardian Angel Home

The Grotto at the Guardian Angel Home

You are cordially invited to the online preview of the book

**Did I Ever Thank You, Sister?**
A True Story

at
www.salsbook.com

Written by Sal N. DiLeo, Edited by Jane E. DiLeo

To receive more information:
tel 612.789.2795    cell 612.207.1109    e-mail: sal@salsbook.com
2611 Ulysses St. NE, Minneapolis, MN 55418

January 29th, 2002 launching of the web site with Sal's Book and Beth's 51st Birthday

Charles R. Di Leo
Born in NY, NY—10/27/38

Angela G. Di Leo
Born in Staten Island, NY—8/8/40

Geralamo (Jerome) A. Di Leo
Born in, Staten Island, NY—8/3/41

Josephine M. Di Leo
Born in Staten Island, NY—6/2/43

Anthony M. Di Leo, Jr.
Born in Rome, NY—12/29/44

Rosario Di Leo
Born in Rome, NY—6/19/46

Michael A. Di Leo
Born in Rome, NY— 6/10/47

Vincent P. Di Leo
Born in Chicago, IL—8/26/49

Mario J. Di Leo
Born in Chicago, IL—8/29/50

Maria A. Di Leo
Born in Potosi, MO—10/18/51
Died: Dec. 21, 1990 · L A, Ca.

Salvatore N. Di Leo
Born in Baldwin, MO—4/12/54

Catherine S. Di Leo
Born in Sparta, IL—12/31/56

Antonio Victorio Emanuelle Di Leo
Born: Ribera, Sicily—Nov. 12, 1912
Died: Rialto, CA—Feb. 22, 1985

Rosaria Josephine Di Leo (Perniciaro)
Born: Greenich Village, NY—Jan. 26, 1919
Died: Erie, PA. —March 16, 1990

## Sal Di Leo's Family Tree

Circa 1920's
My Mother's cousin Santa on left,
and my Mother. Age 7

My Mothers cousin Santa and my Mother
At Confirmation

Katherine and Mose Perniciaro
My Mother's step Mother and
Father
At my Mothers Wedding 1937

Santa and my Mother
Age 17
Catholic Girls School

The family pastry shop Greenwich Village, New York.
Circa 1930's
(Behind the counter on the left) My mother's father Mose'
and her mother Catherine.
(Right) My mother's aunt, uncle and unknown young man behind counter.

This is the home my mother's father and uncle built on the ocean.
My mother spent all of her summers there as a young woman.
Circa 1930's

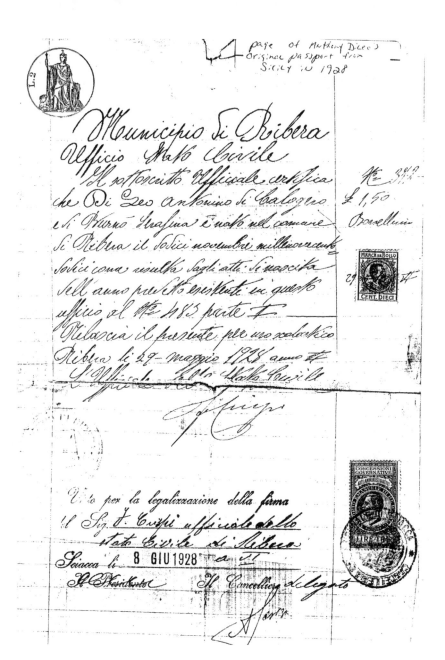

Copy of my Fathers original Passport 1928
A Sicilian Citizen

155

My Fathers Mother, Sarafino (Burno) Di Leo
Circa 1930's
With unknown Child

My Father's Father, Calogero Di Leo
Circa 1930's
With unknown child

My Father
Anthony Di Leo
In his later years.

Di Leo Family Christmas
1957

Di Leo Family Christmas Reunion
1989

Di Leo Family Christmas Reunion
1989
My Sister Maria as a Catholic Nun

# IN MEMORY

Ann Magruder
My high school sweetheart.
1954-2001

Graduation Day
June of 1972
Boystown Nebraska

Sal in front row,"Unit". Able Hall 8th floor gang,"The Hebes" 1976, Univeristy of Nebraska.

163

The rest of the Able Hall 8th floor gang, "The Hebes" 1976, University of Nebraska

Leach Avenue
Joliet, IL
The last home we lived in when my Father ran off.
38 years later.

Anita and her Mother Santa Isola, my Mother's
cousin and her Daughter.
February 2001

Kitty and Sal
1965
On the front steps of the Guardian Angel Home

Sal on the same steps 35 years later.

# With Special Appreciation To Our Friends...

If you truly liked this story, would you please tell others about it.

Thank you,

Sal Di Leo